PENGUIN BOOKS — ENGLISH JOURNEYS

One Green Field

ONE
GREEN
FIELD

Edward
Thomas

English 🐧 *Journeys*

PENGUIN BOOKS

Published by the Penguin Group
Penguin Books Ltd, 80 Strand, London WC2R ORL, England
Penguin Group (USA) Inc., 375 Hudson Street, New York, New York 10014, USA
Penguin Group (Canada), 90 Eglinton Avenue East, Suite 700, Toronto, Ontario, Canada M4P 2Y3
(a division of Pearson Penguin Canada Inc.)
Penguin Ireland, 25 St Stephen's Green, Dublin 2, Ireland
(a division of Penguin Books Ltd)
Penguin Group (Australia), 250 Camberwell Road, Camberwell, Victoria 3124, Australia
(a division of Pearson Australia Group Pty Ltd)
Penguin Books India Pvt Ltd, 11 Community Centre, Panchsheel Park, New Delhi – 110 017, India
Penguin Group (NZ), 67 Apollo Drive, Rosedale, North Shore 0632, New Zealand
(a division of Pearson New Zealand Ltd)
Penguin Books (South Africa) (Pty) Ltd, 24 Sturdee Avenue, Rosebank, Johannesburg 2196, South Africa

Penguin Books Ltd, Registered Offices: 80 Strand, London WC2R ORL, England

www.penguin.com

This selection of pieces is taken from *The Heart of England* (1906), except for 'Spring on
the Pilgrims' Way' and 'June – Hampshire – The Golden Age – Traherne' which are taken
from *The South Country* (1906)
Published in Penguin Books 2009

006

All rights reserved

Set by Rowland Phototypesetting Ltd, Bury St Edmunds, Suffolk
Printed in England by Clays Ltd, St Ives plc

978–0–141–19091–4

www.greenpenguin.co.uk

Penguin Books is committed to a sustainable
future for our business, our readers and our planet.
This book is made from Forest Stewardship
Council™ certified paper.

MIX
Paper from
responsible sources
FSC
www.fsc.org   FSC™ C018179

ALWAYS LEARNING   **PEARSON**

Contents

1. *Spring on the Pilgrims' Way*

Even the motor road is pleasant now when the nightingales sing out of the bluebell thickets under oak and sweet chestnut and hornbeam and hazel. Presently it crosses a common, too small ever to draw a crowd, a rough up-and-down expanse of gorse and thorn, pierced by grassy paths and surrounded by turf that is rushy and mounded by old ant heaps; and here, too, there are nightingales singing alone, the sweeter for the contrast between their tangled silent bowers and the sharp, straight white road. The common is typical of the lesser commons of the south. Crouch's Croft in Sussex is another, in sight of the three dusk moorland breasts of Crowborough; gorse-grown, flat, possessing a pond, and walled by tall hollies in a hedge. Piet Down, close by, is a fellow to it – grass and gorse and irregular pine – a pond, too – rough, like a fragment of Ashdown or Woolmer, and bringing a wild sharp flavour into the mellow cultivated land. Yet another is at Stone Street, very small, a few oaks up to their knees in blackthorn, gorse and bramble, with dusty edge and the hum of the telegraph wire for a song.

After the little common and long meadows, oak and ash, an old stone house with seven hundred years of history quiet within its walls and dark tiles – its cedar and yew and pine, its daisied grass, its dark water and swans – the four oast cones opposite, all taste more exquisitely. How goodly are the names hereabout! – Dinas Dene, the coombe in which the old house stands; Balk Shaw, Cream Crox, Dicky May's Field, Ivy Hatch, Lady Lands, Lady's Wood, Upper and Lower Robsacks, Obram Wood, Ruffats, Styant's Mead, the Shode, and, of course, a Starvecrow. Almost due west goes one of the best of footpaths past hop garden, corn, currant plantations, rough copses, with glimpses of the immense Weald to the east, its trees massed like thirty miles of wood, having sky and cloud over its horizon as if over sea, and southward the wild ridge of Ashdown. Then the path enters tall woods of ash and oak, boulder-strewn among their anemone and primrose, bluebell and dog's mercury, and emerges in a steep lane at the top of which are five cowled oast houses among cherry blossom and under black firs. Beyond there is a hollow winding vale of meadow and corn, its sides clothed in oak, hazel and thorn, revealing primroses between. Woods shut it away from the road and from all houses but the farm above one end. A few cattle graze there, and the sun comes through the sloping woods and makes the grass golden or pale.

Then the North Downs come in sight, above a church tower amid stateliest pale-foliaged beeches and vast undulations of meadow. They are suffused in late sunshine, their trees misty and massed, under a happy sky. Those beeches lie below the road, lining the edge of one long meadow. The opposite sun pours almost horizontal beams down upon the perfectly new leaves so as to give each one a yellow-green glow and to some a silver shimmer about the shadowy boles. For the moment the trees lose their anchor in the solid earth. They are floating, wavering, shimmering, more aerial and pure and wild than birds or any visible things, than aught except music and the fantasies of the brain. The mind takes flight and hovers among the leaves with whatsoever powers it has akin to dew and trembling lark's song and rippling water; it is throbbed away not only above the ponderous earth but below the firmament in the middle world of footless fancies and half thoughts that drift hither and thither and know neither a heaven nor a home. It is a loss of a name and not of a belief that forbids us to say to-day that sprites flutter and tempt there among the new leaves of the beeches in the late May light.

Almost every group of oast houses here, seen either amongst autumn fruit or spring blossom, is equal in its effect to a temple, though different far, even when ivy-mantled as they occasionally are, from the grey towered or spired churches standing near. The low round brick tower of the oast house, surmounted by a tiled cone of about equal height, and that again crested with a white cowl and vane, is a pleasant form. There are groups of three which, in their age, mellow hue, roundness, and rustic dignity, have suggested the triple mother goddesses of old religions who were depicted as matrons, carrying babes or fruit or flowers, to whom the peasant brought thank-offerings when sun and rain had been kind. Those at Kemsing, for example, stand worthily beside the perfect grey-shingled spire, among elm and damson, against the bare cloudy Down. And there are many others near the Pilgrims' Way of the same charm.

That road, in its winding course from Winchester to Canterbury, through Hampshire, Surrey and Kent, sums up all qualities of roads except those of the straight highway. It is a cartway from farm to farm; or a footpath only, or a sheaf of half a dozen footpaths worn side by side; or, no longer needed except by the curious, it is buried under nettle and burdock and barricaded by thorns and traveller's joy and bryony bines; it has been converted into a white country road for a few miles of its length, until an ascent over the Downs or a descent into the valley has to be made, and then once more it is left to footsteps upon grass and bird's-foot trefoil or to rude wheels over flints. Sometimes it is hidden among untended hazels or among chalk banks topped with beech and yew, and the kestrel plucks the chaffinch there undisturbed. Or it goes free and hedgeless like a long balcony half-way up the Downs, and unespied it beholds half the South Country between ash-tree boles. Church and inn and farm and cottage and tramp's fire it passes like a wandering wraith of road. Some one of the little gods of the earth has kept it safe – one of those little and less than omnipotent gods who, neglecting all but their own realms, enjoy the earth in narrow ways, delighting to make small things fair, such as a group of trees, a single field, a pure pool of sedge and bright water, an arm of sea, a train of clouds, a road. I see their hands in many a by-way of space and moment of time. One of them assuredly harbours in a rude wet field I know of that lies neglected between two large estates: three acres at most of roughly sloping pasture, bounded above by the brambly edge of a wood and below by a wild stream. Here a company of meadow-sweet invades the grass, there willow herb tall with rosy summits of flowers, hoary lilac mint, dull golden fleabane, spiry coltstails. The snake creeps careless through these thickets of bloom. The sedge-warbler sings there. One old white horse is content with the field, summer and winter, and has made a plot of it silver with his hairs where he lies at night. The image of the god is in the grey riven willow that leans leafless over the stream like a peasant sculpture of old time. There is another of these godkins in a bare chalk hollow where the dead thistles stick out through a yard of snow and give strange thoughts of the sailless beautiful sea that once rippled over the Downs: one also in the smell of hay and mixen and cow's breath at the first farm out of London where the country is unsoiled. There is one in many a worthless waste by the roadside, such as that between two roads that go almost parallel for a while – a long steep piece, only a few feet broad, impenetrably overgrown by blackthorn and blackberry, but unenclosed: and one in each of the wayside chalk-pits with overhanging beech roots above and bramble below. One, too, perhaps many, were abroad one August night on a high hillside when the hedge crickets sang high up in the dogwood and clematis like small but deafening sewing machines, and the glowworms shone in the thyme, and the owl's crying did not rend the breathless silence under the full moon, and in the confused moonlit chequer of the wood, where tree and shadow were equals, I walked on a grating of shadows with lights between as if from under the earth; the hill was given over to a light happiness through which I passed an unwilling but unfeared intruder.

In places these gods preside over some harmony of the earth with the works of men. There is one such upon the Pilgrims' Way, where I join it, after passing the dark boughs and lightsome flowers of cherry orchards, grass full of dandelions, a dark cluster of pines, elms in groups and cavalcades, and wet willowy meadows that feed the Medway. Just at the approach there is a two-storied farm with dormers in the darkly mellowed roof, protected by sycamores and chestnuts, and before it a weather-boarded barn with thatched roof, and then, but not at right angles, another with ochre tiles, and other outbuildings of old brick and tile, a wagon lodge of flint and thatch beside a pond, at the edge of a broad unhedged field where random oaks shadow the grass. Behind runs the Pilgrims' Way, invisible but easily guessed under that line of white beam and yew, with here and there an ash up which the stout plaited stems of ivy are sculptured, for they seem of the same material as the tree, and both of stone. Under the yew and white beam the clematis clambers over dogwood and wayfaring trees. Corn grows up to the road and sometimes hops; beyond, a league of orchard is a-froth round farmhouses or islands of oak; and east and west sweeps the crescent of the North Downs.

With the crescent goes the road, half-way up the sides of the hills but nearly always at the foot of the steepest slopes where the chalk-pits are carved white, like the concave of a scallop shell, out of the green turf. Luxuriant hedges bar the view except at gateways and stiles. At one place the upper hedge gives way to scattered thickets scrambling up the hill, with chalky ruts and rabbit workings between. Neither sheep nor crops cover the hill, nor yet is it common. Any one can possess it – for an hour. It is given up to the rabbits until Londoners can be persuaded to build houses on it. At intervals a road as old as the Way itself descends precipitously in a deep chalk groove, overhung by yew and beech, or hornbeam, or oak, and white clouds drifting in a river of blue sky between the trees; and joins farther south the main road which winds, parallel with the Pilgrims' Way and usually south of it, from Winchester, through Guildford, Dorking, Westerham, Maidstone, Ashford, and Canterbury to Dover Strait. Not only chalk-pits and deep roads hollow the hills. For miles there is a succession of small smooth coombes, some grown with white thorn, some grassy, above the road, alternating with corresponding smooth breasts of turf. Towers and spires, but chiefly towers, lie beneath, and in the mile or so between one and the next there are red farms or, very rarely, a greater house at the end of a long wave of grass among trees. Above, the white full-bosomed clouds lean upon the green rampart of the hills and look across to the orchards, the woods beyond, the oaken Weald and its lesser ridges still farther, and then the South Downs and a dream of the south sea.

Rain falls, and in upright grey sheaves passes slowly before the fresh beech leaves like ghosts in shadowy procession; and once again the white clouds roll over the tops of the trees, and the green is virginal, and out of the drip and glimmer of the miles of blissful country rises the blackbird's song and the cuckoo's shout. The rain seems not only to have brightened what is to be seen but the eye that sees and the mind that knows, and suddenly we are aware of all the joy in the grandeur and mastery of an oak's balance, in those immobile clouds revealed on the farthest horizon shaped like the mountains which a child imagines, in the white candles of the beam tree, in the black-eyed bird sitting in her nest in the hawthorn with uplifted beak, and in the myriad luxuriant variety of shape and texture and bright colour in the divided leaves of wood sanicle and moschatel and parsley and cranesbill, in the pure outline of twayblade and violet and garlic. Newly dressed in the crystal of the rain the landscape recalls the earlier spring; the flowers of white wood-sorrel, the pink and white anemone and cuckoo flower, the thick-clustered, long-stalked primroses and darker cowslips with their scentless sweetness pure as an infant's breath; the solitary wild cherry trees flowering among still leafless beech; the blackbirds of twilight and the flower-faced owls; the pewits wheeling after dusk; the jonquil and daffodil and arabis and leopard's bane of cottage gardens; the white clouds plunged in blue floating over the brown woods of the hills; the delicate thrushes with speckled breasts paler than their backs, motionless on dewy turf; and all the joys of life that come through the nostrils from the dark, not understood world which is unbolted for us by the delicate and savage fragrances of leaf and flower and grass and clod, of the plumage of birds and fur of animals and breath and hair of women and children.

How can our thoughts, the movements of our bodies, our human kindnesses, ever fit themselves with this blithe world? Is it but vain remorse at what is lost, or is it not rather a token of what may yet be achieved, that makes these images blind us as does the sight of children dressed for a play, some solemn-thoughtful, some wholly gay, suddenly revealed to us in brilliant light after the night wind and rain?

But at morning twilight I see the moon low in the west like a broken and dinted shield of silver hanging long forgotten outside the tent of a great knight in a wood, and inside are the knight's bones clean and white about his rusted sword. In the east the sun rises, a red-faced drover and a million sheep going before him silent over the blue downs of the dawn: and I am ill-content and must watch for a while the fraying, changeful edges of the lesser clouds drift past and into the great white ones above, or hear rebellious music that puts for one brief hour into our hands the reins of the world that we may sit mightily behind the horses and drive to the goal of our dreams.

A footpath leads from the Pilgrims' Way past the divine undulations and beech glades of a park – a broad piece of the earth that flows hither and thither in curves, sudden or slow but flawless and continuous, and everywhere clothed in a seamless garment of grass. The path crosses the white main road into a lesser one that traverses a common of beech and oak and birch. The leaves make an unbroken roof over the common: except the roads there is not a path in it. For it is a small and narrow strip of but a few acres, without any open space, gloomy, much overgrown by thickets. Last year's leaves lie undisturbed and of the colour of red deer under the silky green new foliage and round the huge mossy pedestals of beech and in caves behind the serpentine locked roots. No child's shout is heard. No lover walks there. The motor-car hurries the undesirable through and down into the Weald. And so it is alone and for themselves that the beeches rise up in carven living stone and expand in a green heaven for the song of the woodwren, pouring out pearls like wine.

Southward, on either side of the steep road, the slope is, below the beeches, given to corn and hops; at the foot are all the oaks and pasture of the Weald, diversified by hop gardens on many of the slanting fields that break up its surface. Looking back from here the hills above are less finely modelled than the downs still farther behind us in the north. But they also have their shallow coombes, sometimes two tiers of them, and they are indented by deep, wide-mouthed bays. One of them begins in copses of oak and hazel and sallow, a little arable, a farm, three oast cones, and a little steep orchard in a hollow of their own, which give way to hops, followed by grass and then a tortuous ploughland among the oaks and firs of the great woods that cover the more precipitous sides of the upper end of the bay. Exquisitely cultivated, this bay is yet a possession of cuckoo and nightingale, singing under the yellow-green and black-branched oaks and above the floor of bluebell and dark dog's mercury.

Out of the coombe a deep lane ascends through beech, hazel and beam to another common of heather, and whinberry bathing the feet of scattered birch, and squat oak and pine, interrupted by yellow gravel pits.

Beyond is a little town and a low grey spire, neighboured by sycamores that stretch out horizontal boughs of broad leaves and new yellow-green flower tassels over long grass. Past the town – rapidly and continually resuming its sleep after the hooting of motor-cars – begins a wide and stately domain. At its edge are cottages doddering with age, but trim and flowery, and assuredly wearing the livery of the ripe, grave house of brick that stands on the grassy ascent above them, among new-leaved beech masses and isolated thorns dreaming over their shadows. That grove of limes, fair and decorous, leading up to the house is the work of Nature and the squire. His chestnut and pine plantations succeed. And now a pollard beech, bossy-rooted on a mound of moss and crumbling earth, its grotesque torso decorated as by childish hands with new leaves hanging among mighty boughs that are themselves a mansion for squirrel and jay and willow wren and many shadows, looks grimly down at the edge of a wood and asks for the wayfarer's passport – has he lived well, does he love this world, is he bold and free and kind? – and if he have it not seals him with melancholy as he enters among the innumerable leaves of innumerable beeches beginning to respond to the straight, still, after-sunset rain, while the last cuckoo's cry and the last footsteps and wheels of the world die away behind. The foliage has a pale, almost white, light of its own among the darkly dripping boughs, and when that is gone the rain and leaf under a spongy grey sky have a myriad voices of contentedness. Below, invisible in the dark rain but not unfelt, is the deep hollow land of the Weald. The owls whimper and mew and croon and hoot and shriek their triumphs.

2. A Decorated Church

Out of the midst of pale wheat lands and tussocky
meadow, intersected by streams which butter-bur and
marigold announce, and soared over by pewit and lark
and the first swallows with their delicate laughter, rises
the grim, decorated church, of the same colour as the
oak trees round about. White and grey headstones, some
of great age, bow to it in the churchyard, and seem
mutely to crave for the shelter from the north-east wind.
There is much room within. All the headstones and
those whom they commemorate might find places and
not crowd out the little congregation. In one transept a
knight and lady are taking their ease in stone, and looking
up at the gaudy arms above them. They came early to
the church. From the memorial inscriptions on pave-
ment and walls, it would seem that the church belongs
to a later great family, still living near. Soldiers, sailors,
landowners, clergymen even, they take possession at
their death; from 1623 they have flocked here, and the
names of their virtues live after them; tyrants perhaps in
their lifetime, they have the air of being idols now, and
they outnumber the prophets on the window glass. The
service proceeds in the accustomed decent manner, with
nasal lesson and humming prayer. Then comes the
hymn:

Through all the changing scenes of life –

One woman's ambitious, shrill treble voice that seems ever about to fall and yet continues to maintain its airy height, leads the congregation to unusual adventures of song. The church is dense with emotion; ordinary gentlemen, shopkeepers, labourers and their wives, men and women of all degrees of endurance, chivalry, good intention, uncertain aims, sentimental virtuousness, hypocrisy not dissevered from hardship, vanity not ignorant of tenderness, hard ambition, the desire to be respected – men and women throw all kinds of strange meaning, heartfelt and present, imaginative, retrospective, expectant, into the vague words of the hymn. I can see one strong man shouting it with an expression as if he were pole-axing a bull. His neighbour, a frail, tearful woman, sings as if it absolves her from the tears with which she marred not only her own life. One aged woman made it clearly an expression of the nothingness of mankind, a ridicule and blasphemy of life, as if she had repeated the words of the old play:

> Where is now Solomon, in wisdom so excellent?
> Where is now Samson, in battle so strong?
> Where is now Absalom, in beauty resplendent?
> Where is now good Jonathan, hid so long?
> Where is now Cæsar, in victory triumphing?
> Where is now Dives, in dishes so dainty?
> Where is now Tully, in eloquence exceeding?
> Where is now Aristotle, learned so deeply?
> What emperors, kings, and dukes in times past,

What earls and lords, and captains of war,
What popes and bishops, all at the last
In the twinkling of an eye are fled so far?
How short a feast is this worldly joying?
Even as a shadow it passeth away,
Depriving a man of gifts everlasting,
Leading to darkness and not to day!
O meat of worms, O heap of dust,
O like to dew, climb not too high.

Other faces express complacency, hope, the newness of a solution of this thing life, grim, satisfied despair, even a kind of vanity. All these men and women might agree at a political meeting; here they differ each from the rest, and every one of the gods in all the mythologies must be gladdened or angered at some part of the hymn by the meaning of this or that worshipper; Odin, Apollo, Diana, Astarte, the Cat, the Beetle, and the rest revive, in whatever Tartarus they are thrust, at these strange sounds.

The last of the congregation left, but I could still hear the hymn wandering feebly among the tall arches and up and about, apparently restless, as if it sought to get out and away, but in vain. The high grey stone and those delicate windows made a cage; and the human voices were as those of Seifelmolouk and his memlooks, when the giant king kept them in cages because the sound of their lamentation seemed to him the most melodious music, and he thought them birds. Inexorably, the fancy held me that some gaunt giant, fifty cubits high, kept men and women in this cage because he loved to hear their voices expressing moods he knew nothing of. Not more caged are the five brown bells in the tower, with mute, patient heads like cows, their names being Solitude, Tranquillity, Duty, Harmony, Joy.

3. An Old Wood

The chestnut blossom is raining steadily and noiselessly down upon a path whose naked pebbles receive mosaic of emerald light from the interlacing boughs. At intervals, once or twice an hour, the wings of a lonely swallow pass that way, when alone the shower stirs from its perpendicular fall. Cool and moist, the perfumed air flows, without lifting the most nervous leaf or letting fall a suspended bead of the night's rain from a honey-suckle bud. In an indefinite sky of grey, through which one ponderous cloud billows into sight and is lost again, no sun shines: yet there is light – I know not whence; for the brass trappings of the horses beam so as to be extinguished in their own fire. There is no song in wood or sky. Some one of summer's wandering voices – bullfinch or willow wren – might be singing, but unheard, at least unrealized. From the dead-nettle spires, with dull green leaves stained by purple and becoming more and more purple towards the crest, which is of a sombre uniform purple, to the elms reposing at the horizon, all things have bowed the head, hushed, settled into a perfect sleep. Those elms are just visible, no more. The path has no sooner emerged from one shade than another succeeds, and so, on and on, the eye wins no broad dominion.

It is a land that uses a soft compulsion upon the

passer-by, a compulsion to meditation, which is necessary before he is attached to a scene rather featureless, to a land that hence owes much of its power to a mood of generous reverie which it bestows. And yet it is a land that gives much. Companionable it is, reassuring to the solitary; he soon has a feeling of ease and seclusion there. The cool-leaved wood! The limitless, unoccupied fields of marsh marigold, seen through the trees, most beautiful when the evening rain falls slowly, dimming and almost putting out the lustrous bloom! Gold of the minute willows underfoot! Leagues of lonely grass where the slow herds tread the daisies and spare them yet!

Towards night, under the sweet rain, at this warm, skyless close of the day, the trees, far off in an indolent, rolling landscape, stand as if disengaged from the world, in a reticent and pensive repose.

But suddenly the rain has ceased. In an old, dense wood the last horizontal beams of the sun embrace the trunks of the trees and they glow red under their moist ceiling of green. A stile to be crossed at its edge, where a little stream, unseen, sways the stiff exuberant angelica that grows from it, gives the word to pause, and with a rush the silence and the solitude fill the brain. The wood is of uncounted age; the ground on which it stands is more ancient than the surrounding fields, for it rises and falls stormily, with huge boulders here and there; not a path intrudes upon it; the undergrowth is impenetrable to all but fox and bird and this cool red light about the trunks of the trees. Far away a gate is loudly shut, and the rich blue evening comes on and severs me irrevocably from all but the light in the old wood and the ghostly white cow-parsley flowers suspended on unseen stalks. And there, among the trees and their shadows, not understood, speaking a forgotten tongue, old dreads and formless awes and fascinations discover themselves and address the comfortable soul, troubling it, recalling to it unremembered years not so long past but that in the end it settles down into a gloomy tranquillity and satisfied discontent, as when we see the place where we were unhappy as children once. Druid and devilish deity and lean wild beast, harmless now, are revolving many memories with me under the strange, sudden red light in the old wood, and not more remote is the league-deep emerald sea-cave from the storm above than I am from the world.

4. *In a Farmyard*

We waited to let the forty cows go past, each of them pausing to lick the forehead of the strawberry cow that leaned over the gate of her stall and lowed continually concerning her newly born white calf. But so slow they were in their wanton, obedient movement to the milking-shed that we turned and found another path, and thus surprised a pond lying deep among tansy flowers, grey nettles, and billows of conquering bramble and brier.

The farmyard was always dusty, or deep with ridgy mire, from the trampling of men and horses and cows in the streets that wound among its cart-lodges, stables, stalls, milking-sheds, and barns all glowing with mature tiles, and ricks gleaming with amber thatch. But in a corner lay unused, older than them all, the long-headed and snaky-bodied pond. We learned to know that pond.

Sometimes, when summer has honoured the water with a perfect suit of emerald green, that pond shows itself to be a monstrous, coiled, primeval thing, lying undisturbed, and content to be still and contemplative. Often has the monster been driven away – by draining; often has it returned, still a green, coiled, primeval being that disappears suddenly in November and leaves a soft, dark pool. Some have ventured to intrude upon the monster, to fish for the sleepy carp which are found when it has been driven from its nest of purple mud; but they fish in vain.

The solitary, dying ash tree at the edge of the pond seems, by day, when the monster is powerful there in the summer, to be but the skeleton of an old victim; or, in the winter, the sad and twisted nymph of the water. But every night, like any dreaming child or musing lover, though not perhaps so happily, is it let into a varied, strange, exalted paradise.

You may see it – on still evenings when the mist prevails over all things except the robin's song, and makes even that more melancholy – or when the songs of many nightingales besiege, enter, and possess the house and the deserted farmyard – or when the cold and entirely silent air under a purple November sky chills the blood, so that friendship and hope and purposes are all in vain as in an opiate dream – then you may see the ash tree take heart. It has the air of one going home upon a lonely road that will not end in loneliness. Those bare and stiff, decaying branches are digits pointing homeward through the sky; the tree forgets the monster at its feet and the children who laugh and the supremacy of the buildings round about. It might seem, with those extended branches, to be a self-torturing and aspiring fanatic who had endured thus for uncounted days and nights, and has his vision at last. For, when night is perfect, the tree exults, and though it is perhaps not joyous, it is as one of those great sorrowful temperaments – of soldier, or explorer, or humorist – so active and inexorable that they may claim kinship with the truly joyous ones. If it is still sad, it is 'endiademed with woe.' How large and satanic it is beside the heavy rounded oaks and the stately, feminine elms and the lovely limes.

Even so might a philosopher heighten and lord it, travelling in Charon's ship along with deflated tyrants and rhetoricians and bold and crimson animals born to eat provinces and to poison worms; even so, Ossian and Arthur and Cuchullain and Achilles triumph over men that were yesterday on thrones and chariots. Often have I seen the tree, and it alone, giving character to the whole valley and filling the land as a bell fills a cathedral or as the droning of a bee fills a lily.

> With him enthroned
> Sat sable-vested night, eldest of things,
> The consort of his reign.

My little thoughts seem to be drawn up among the black branches like twittering birds going to rest in some high cliff that is a chief pillar of the fabric of the night. Half dead and threatened though it be, surely the spirit of it, which is to many a broad and tragical night as the arm of a great painter to his picture, will survive not only me and my words but the tree itself. I have approached it on some moonlit midnights, when the sky was so deep that the tall oaks were as weeds at the bottom of an unfathomed sea, and it has stood up erect and puissant, as if it were the dreamer at one with all he sees, in a world of blind men with open eyes. Then, as the autumn dawn arrived it was still looking towards Orion; defrauded, indeed, for a time of its vision, but not of its glory. The swaying cows wandered to the milking-sheds. The little bats ran to and fro in the air and made their little snipping and drumming sounds. It was light; but the ash tree was not utterly cast down; it still walked in the way of the stars; it was inscribed in solemn characters upon the sun that rose up red in the mist.

5. Meadowland

This is one of the tracts of country which are discovered by few except such as study the railway maps of England in order to know what to avoid. On those maps it is one of several large triangular sections which railways bound, but have not entered. All day long the engines scream along their boundaries, and at night wave fiery arms to the sky, as if to defend a forbidden place or a sanctuary. Within there is peace, and a long ancient lane explores it, with many windings and turnings back, as if it were a humble, diffident inquirer, fortunately creeping on, aiming at some kind of truth and not success, yet without knowing what truth is when he starts. Here it hesitates by a little pool, haunted, as is clear from the scribbled footprints on the shore, only by moorhen and wagtail, and, in the spindle trees beside it, by a witty thrush; there it goes joyously forward, straight among lines of tall oaks and compact thorns; then it turns to climb a hill from which all the country it has passed is visible first, meadow and withy copse and stream, and next the country which it has yet to pass – a simple dairy land with green grass, green woods, and stout grey haystacks round the pale farms. But in a little while it winds, confused again under high maple and dogwood hedges, downhill, as if it had already forgotten what the hilltop showed. On the level again the hollow wood which the willow wren fills with his little lonely song has to be penetrated; the farmyard must be passed through, and the spirit of the road looks in at the dairy window and sees the white disks of cream in the pans and the cool-armed maid lifting a cheese; and yet another farmyard it loiters in, watching the roses and plume-poppy and lupin of the front garden, going between the stables and the barn, and there spreading out as if it had resolved to cease and always watch the idle wagon, the fair-curved hay-rakes leaning against the wall, and the fowls which are the embodiment of senseless reverie – when lo! the path goes straight across wide and level pastures, with a stream at its side. Seen afar off, losing itself among the elms that watch over the hillside church, the little white road is as some quiet, hermit saint, just returned from long seclusion, and about to take up his home for ever and ever in the chancel; but when we reach the place, he is still as far away, still uncertain in the midst of the corn below. At the charlock-yellow summit the road seems to lead into the sky, where the white ladders are let down from the sun.

The ways of such a road – when the June grass is high and in the sun it is invisible except for its blueness and its buttercups, and the chaffinch, the corn-bunting, and yellow-hammer, the sleepiest-voiced birds, are most persistent – easily persuade the mind that it alone is travelling, travelling through an ideal country, belonging to itself and beyond the power of the world to destroy. The few people whom we see, the mower, the man hoeing his onion-bed in a spare half-hour at midday, the children playing 'Jar-jar-winkle' against a wall, the women hanging out clothes – these the very loneliness of the road has prepared us for turning into creatures of dream; it costs an effort to pass the time of day with them, and they being equally unused to strange faces are not loquacious, and so the moment they are passed they are no more real than the men and women of pastoral:

> He leads his Wench a Country Horn-pipe Round,
> About a May-pole on a Holy-day;
> Kissing his lovely Lasse (with Garlands Crownd)
> With whooping heigh-ho singing Care away;
> Thus doth he passe the merry month of May:
>   And all th' yere after in delight and joy,
>   (Scorning a King) he cares for no annoy.

The most credible inhabitants are Mertilla, Florimel, Corin, Amaryllis, Dorilus, Doron, Daphnis, Silvia, and Aminta, and shepherds singing to their flocks

> Lays of sweet love and youth's delightful heat.

Yonder the road curves languidly between hedges and broad fringes of green, and along it an old man guides the cattle in to afternoon milking. They linger to crop the wayside grass and he waits, but suddenly resumes his walk and they obey, now hastening with tight udders and looking from side to side. They turn under the archway of a ruined abbey, and low as if they enjoy the reverberation, and disappear. I never see them again; but the ease, the remoteness, the colour of the red cattle in the green road, the slowness of the old cowman, the timelessness of that gradual movement under the fourteenth-century arch, never vanish.

Of such things the day is made, not of milestones and antiquities. Isolated, rapt from the earth, perhaps, by the very fatigue which at the end restores us to it forcibly, the mind goes on seeing and remembering these things.

Here the cattle stand at the edge of a pond and the tench swim slowly above the weeds amongst them as they stand. The sun strikes down upon the glassy water, but cannot take away the coolness of the reeds about the margin. Under the one oak in the meadow above, the farmer sits with his dog, so still that the dabchick does not dive and the water vole nibbles the reed, making a small sound, the only one.

There five little girls play the lovers' game on a green in front of their cottages. One of them kneels down and cries quietly; the others hold hands and circle round her, singing:

Poor Mary sits a-weeping, a-weeping, a-weeping,
Poor Mary sits a-weeping, by the bright shining shore.

Oh tell us what you're weeping for, weeping for,
    weeping for,
Oh tell us what you're weeping for, by the bright
    shining shore.

Then the little 'poor Mary,' with her face still in her apron, takes up the singing, the others still moving round her:

I'm weeping for my true love, my true love, my true
  love,
I'm weeping for my true love, by the bright shining
  shore.

Then the others sing to her:

Get up and choose a better one, a better one, a better
  one,
Get up and choose a better one, by the bright shining
  shore.

At this, Mary rises, and chooses one of those from the
ring, and the two stand in the middle, holding each
others' hands crossed, while the others sing:

Your true love is a shepherd's cross, a shepherd's cross
  a shepherd's cross,
Your true love is a shepherd's cross, by the bright
  shining shore.

So Mary now takes her place in the ring; her true love
becomes 'poor Mary,' and chooses another lover amidst
the same song; and at last, when all have been Marys
and true lovers, with resolute faces, they scatter care-
lessly and forget. Finding some marbles in a roadside
crevice, I ask one child to play, but she says that marbles
are not played after Good Friday. A white cow rests
beside, so much in love with peace that it grazes lying
down. On the other side of the road the bacon hisses
and smells from a farmhouse whose mountainous thatch

makes a cool cave of tranquillity; on the sunny slope the starlings who have honeycombed the thatch, whistle or creep in with food or straw. Not one path disturbs the unfrequented verdure of the green, though the road winds lazily round it.

Yonder, up a steep field, goes a boy birdnesting in a double hedge, stooping to the nettles for the white throat's eggs, straining high among the hawthorns for a dove's. He does not hasten. Now and then he calls 'cuckoo,' not a timorous note, but lusty like the bird's own: and now he lies down to suck a thrush's egg. He will not take the robin's eggs, 'or I shall get my arm broken,' he says. A cruel game, but so long as he loves it with all his heart perhaps it is forgiven him, and in a few years he will never again go slowly up that field, forgetful of schoolmaster, father and mother, and the greatness of man.

At noon there is a hamlet in front. On one side of it the church thrusts a golden weathercock high into the blue sky, and with his proud and jolly head uplifted towards the north the bird flames and exults; on the other side, tall beeches give out the sleepy noise of rooks. Straight ahead 'The White Hart,' a white inn with heavy, overhanging thatch, divides the road in two. Those white walls can never cease to glow; they have persuaded the sun to sleep under those eaves for ever like the carter on the bench. The sign-board hangs silent, but the sign has melted away. A wagon stands by the door; the wagoner holds a chestnut mare with one hand, with the other he slowly tilts the glittering tankard and shows all of his brown throat throbbing; the hostess watches.

The low white kitchen is cut in two by a tall, semi-circular settle, to which the hostess returns and with a round elm table between her and the fire she lops fine greens into a pail. A tenanted fireplace is better than a cold one on any day of the year, and it is cool in the window seat between the ale and the wind. Outside lies the little road, waiting for me. And now we go on together, the road having still the advantage of me, though it has poured no libation.

All through the long afternoon that land offers symbols of peace, security, and everlastingness. Tall hedges half hidden in a rising tide of long, starry herbage, ponds where the probing carp make the lily leaves rise and flap, wide meadows where the cows wander half a mile an hour, vast green cumulus clouds with round summits here and there disclosing infinite receding glooms of blue – these with their continual presence store the mind, giving it not only that poignant joy in which half consciously we know that never again shall we be just here and thus, but the joy, too, of knowing that we take these things along with us to the end –

> Then whate'er
> Poor laws divide the public year,
> Whose revolutions wait upon
> The wild turns of the wanton sun;
> There all the year is love's long spring,
> There all the year love's nightingales shall sit and sing.

On that poem of Crashaw's to his ivory-handed mistress runs my thought as the road, towards evening, once more progresses without any hedges between it and the fields, when a broad double hedge or narrow copse of oak and ash departs at a right angle from the way. Up to the briers and thorns at the hem of the trees comes the close, cool yellow grass and obtains a shadow there. Out on to that grass the blackbirds have strayed and are straying farther and farther; the rabbits, too, are well away from shelter, hopping a few steps and crouching. In the hedge itself a hedge-sparrow just once lets loose its frail dewy song, a nightingale utters one phrase of marvelling and is still. The musky wild roses star all the hedge and the scent begins to wander in the moist air with the scent of honeysuckle and of shadowy grasses. Under a now misted sky that makes the light seem to dwell no longer in it but in the grass, the flat, yellow field running to the little wood is a place impregnable and inaccessible. Invisible walls shut me off, though no hedge intervenes; no dreadful barrier could do it more effectually. It would be as easy to step into the past as into this candid field, a withdrawn world with its own sun.

A mile farther a little town stands upon the edge of this enclosed land. A brook runs down to its edge and half encircles it. Clean and fair, shining with linen, the meadows come right up to the town which turns its back upon them, with long rows of beans and peas dividing the yellow houses from one another. The chimney smoke rises above the criss-cross roofs of stone and thatch and then travels round the church tower, which emerges from the houses like some grave schoolmaster out of his children, most of them thronging close and others wandering, in wedge or line, into the fields. In the town the road loses itself, bewildered among islands made by inns and groups of cottages, the church and the shops. Among these pour a flock of sheep, swelling as the streets enlarge, contracting as they contract, and always filling them. Within the town there is not a blade of grass, nor a garden, nor a tree; and yet the richly burning roofs, the grey or white walls, the sign of 'The Spotted Cow,' or the sign of 'The Sun,' make not an interruption but a diversion in the fields, when suddenly, between two white walls, shines the green evening land, and across it a busy train rushes and vanishes with long, delicious, dying reverberations among the dark woods and rosy clouds at the horizon.

6. Poppies

The earliest mower had not risen yet; the only sign of human life was the light that burned all night in a cottage bedroom, here and there; and from garden to garden went the white owl with that indolent flight which seems ever about to cease, and he seemed to be the disembodied soul of a sleeper, vague, homeless, wandering, softly taking a dim joy in all the misty, dense forget-me-not, pansy, cornflower, Jacob's ladder, wallflower, love-in-a-mist, and rose of the borders, before the day of work once more began.

So I followed the owl across the green and past the church until I came to the deserted farm. There the high-porched barn, the doorless stables, the cumbered stalls, the decaying house, received something of life from the owl, from the kind twilight, or from my working mind. Above the little belfry on the housetop the flying fox of the weather-vane was still, fixed for ever by old age in the south, recording not the hateful east, the crude and violent north, the rainy west wind. Whether because the buildings bore upon their surfaces the marks of many generations of life, all harmoniously continuous, or whether because though dead and useless they yet seemed to enjoy and could speak to a human spirit, I do not know, but I could fancy that, unaided, they were capable of inspiring afresh the idea of immortality to one who desired it. Mosses grew on the old tiles and were like moles for softness and rotundity. A wind that elsewhere made no sound talked meditatively among the timbers. The village Maypole, transported there a generation ago, stood now as a flagstaff in the yard, and had it burst into leaf and flower it would hardly have surprised. Billows of tall, thick nettle, against the walls and in every corner, were a luxuriant emblem of all the old careless ease of the labourers who, despite their sweat and anxiety and hopelessness, yet had time to lean upon their plough or scythe or hoe to watch the hounds or a carriage go by. Tall tansy and fleabane and hawkweeds and dandelions, yellow blossoms, stood for the bright joys of the old life. The campions on the hedge, the fumitory in the kitchen garden, meant the vague moods between sorrow and joy, speaking of them as clearly as when from out of the church flows the litany, charged with the emotion of those who hear it not, though lying near. Had the wise owner admitted these things and for their sake obeyed the command of the will which bade him leave the Green Farm untouched? He might well have done so had he seen the birth of colour after colour in the dawn.

At first, when doves began to coo and late cuckoos to call in invisible woods beyond, I thought that the green of grass was alive again; but that was only because I knew it was grass and could translate its grey. The green trees were still black above a lake of white mist far off when the yellows of hawkweed and tansy rose up. The purple fumitory, the blue of speedwells, came later. And then, as I turned a shadowy corner and came out into the broad half-light just before sunrise, I saw the crimson of innumerable poppies that had a thought of mist pearl enmeshed amongst them.

They were not fifty yards away – they were in a well-known place – and yet there towered high walls and gloomed impassable moats between them and me, such was the strangeness of their beauty. Had they been reported to me from Italy or the East, had I read of them on a supreme poet's page, they could not have been more remote, more inaccessible, more desirable in their serenity. Something in me desired them, might even seem to have long ago possessed and lost them, but when thought followed vision as, alas! it did, I could not understand their importance, their distance from my mind, their desirableness, as of a far-away princess to a troubadour. They were stranger than the high stars, as beautiful as any woman new-born out of summer air, though I could have reaped them all in half an hour. A book in a foreign, unknown language which is known to be full of excellent things is a simple possession and untantalizing compared with these. They proposed impossible dreams of strength, health, wisdom, beauty, passion – could I but relate myself to them more closely than by wonder, as a child to a ship at sea which, after all, he may one day sail in, or of a lover for one whom he may some day attain. I was glad and yet I fatigued myself by a gladness so inhuman. Did men, I asked myself, once upon a time have simply an uplifting of the heart at a sight like this? Or were they destined in the end to come to that – a blissful end? Had I offended against the commonwealth of living things that I was not admitted as an equal to these flowers? Why could they not have vanished and left me with my first vision, instead of staying and repeating that it would be as easy to draw near to the stars as to them?

And yet the mind is glad, if it is troubled, of an impossible, far-away princess. She deceives the mind as Columbus deceived his weary sailors by giving out at the end of each day fewer knots than they had truly travelled, in order that they should not lose courage at the immensity of the voyage.

And still the poppies shone and the blackbird sang from his tower of ivory.

7. *August*

I have found only two satisfying places in the world in August – the Bodleian Library and a little reedy, willowy pond, where you may enjoy the month perfectly, sitting and being friendly with moorhen and kingfisher and snake, except in the slowly recurring intervals when you catch a tench and cast only mildly envious eyes upon its cool, olive sides. Through the willows I see the hot air quiver in crystal ripples like the points of swords, and sometimes I see a crimson cyclist on a gate. Thus is 'fantastic summer's heat' divine. For in August it is right to be cool and at the same time to enjoy the sight and perfume of heat out of doors. In June and July the frosts and east winds of May are so near in memory that they give a satisfaction to the sensation of heat. In September frosts and east winds return. August, in short, is the month of Nature's perfect poise, and I should like to see it represented in painting by a Junonian woman, immobile, passionless, and happy in a cool-leaved wood, and looking neither forward nor backward, but within.

Far off I see a forest-covered hill that says 'Peace' with a great, quiet voice. From the pool and towards the hill runs a shining road, with some of its curves visible for miles, which I have not followed and dare not follow, because it seems to lead to the Happy Fields.

Between the pool and the road is a house built squarely of white stone. A tiled roof, where the light is always mellow as sunset in the various hues that sometimes mix and make old gold, slopes from the many-angled chimneys and juts out beyond and below the wall of the house. In that shadowy pocket of the eaves the martins build, and on a day of diamond air their shadows are as rivulets upon the white wall. Four large windows frame a cool and velvety and impenetrable gloom. Between them stand four still cypresses.

A footpath skirts the pool, and on one side tall grasses rise up, on the other thorns and still more grasses, heavy with flowers and the weight of birds. The grasses almost meet across the path, and a little way ahead mix in a mist through which the whitethroat and the dragon-fly climb or descend continually. The little green worlds below the meeting grasses are full of the music of bright insects and the glow of flowers. The long stems ascend in the most perfect grace; pale green, cool, and pleasant to the touch, stately and apparently full of strength, with a certain benignity of shape that is pleasant to the eye and mind. Branched, feathered, and tufted heads of flower top the tall grass, and in the clear air each filament divides itself from the rest as the locks of the river-moss divide on the water's flow. All bend in trembling curves with their own fullness, and the butterflies crown them from time to time. When wind plays with the perfectly level surface of the grasses their colours close in and part and knit arabesques in the path of the light sand martins. Sometimes the mailed insects creep along the pennons of the grass leaves to sun themselves, other insects visit the forget-me-nots in the pool. Every plant has its miniature dryad.

Nearer, and sometimes in the water, the branched meadow-sweet mingles the foam of its blossom and the profuse verdure of its leaves with willow herb, blue brooklime, white cresses, and the dark purple figwort. A mellow red, like that of autumn oaks or hawthorn at the first touch of spring, tinges the meadow-sweet. The disposition of its flowers is so exquisite that they seem to have been moulded to the shape of some delicate hand; every bud takes part in the effect. The lithe meanders of the stems are contrasted with the intricacy of the goose-grass and the contortion of the forget-me-nots. Both in the midst of the long stalk and in the plume of flowers the branching is so fine and the curves rely so intimately upon one another that a simple copy on paper is cool and pensive after the vanity of cultivated curiousness. Hardly anywhere is there a visible shadow; at most there is a strange tempering of pure light that throws a delicate bloom upon the cattle and the birds, and a kind of seriousness upon the face or flower within its influence. A dark insect of clear wings alights upon the new hawkweed flower, and sits probing deliciously in its deep heart; but, although the petals are in the midst of grasses and under thorns, the fly perches unshadowed, and throws no shade beyond a moistening of the flower's gold. The close purple flowers of the vetches are scarcely duller in the recesses, where the plant begins to climb, than at the summit where the buds bear a fine down. The fish gleam deep in the pool. The dark ivy shines in the innermost parts of the wood.

But these are merely the things that I see beside the pool, and here, more than anywhere else, the things that are seen are the least important. For they are but the fragments of the things that are embroidered on the hem of a great garment, which gathers the clouds and mountains in its folds; and in the hair of the wearer hang the stars, braided and whorled in patterns too intricate for our eyes. The Junonian woman is a little ivory image of the figure which I think of by the pool. She is older than the pool and the craggy oak at its edge, as old as the stars. But to-day she has taken upon herself the likeness of one who is a girl for lightness and joy, a woman for wisdom, a goddess for calm. Last month she seemed to laugh and dance. Next month she will seem to have grey in her hair. To-day she is perfect.

8. *One Green Field*

Happiness is not to be pursued, though pleasure may be; but I have long thought that I should recognize happiness could I ever achieve it. It would be health, or at least unthwarted intensity of sensual and mental life, in the midst of beautiful or astonishing things which should give that life full play and banish expectation and recollection. I never achieved it, and am fated to be almost happy in many different circumstances, and on account of my forethought to be contemptuous or even disgusted at what the beneficent designs of chance have brought – refusing, for example, to abandon my nostrils frankly to the 'musk and amber' of revenge; or polluting, by the notice of some trivial accident, the remembrance of past things, both bitter and sweet, in the company of an old friend. Wilfully and yet helplessly I coin mere pleasures out of happiness. And yet herein, perhaps, a just judge would declare me to be at least not more foolish than those men who are always pointing out the opportunities and just causes of happiness which others have. Also, the flaw in my happiness which wastes it to a pleasure is in the manner of my looking back at it when it is past. It is as if I had made a great joyous leap over a hedge, and then had looked back and seen that the hedge was but four feet high and not dangerous. Is it perhaps true that those are never happy who know what happiness is? The shadow of it I seem to see every day in entering a little idle field in a sternly luxuriant country.

It is but five grassy acres, and yet as the stile admitting you to it makes you pause – to taste the blackberries or to see how far the bryony has twined – you salute it in a little while as a thing of character. Many of the fields around are bounded by straight-ruled hedges, as if they had been cut up by a tyrant or a slave, with only a few of such irregularities as a stream or a pond may enforce. Not one of the five hedges of this field makes a straight line. The hedge up to your right from the stile is of a noble and fascinating unruliness. So winds a mountain stream down its ladders of crag in Cardigan; into some such form would the edge of a phalanx be worn by long swaying in the height of battle. The other hedges are equally fretted. Here, there is a deep indentation where the cattle lie and wear the blackthorn stems until they are polished for ever; and there the knitted stoles and roots of ash jut out and encroach, fierce and antique and stony, like a strange beast left there to lie in the sweet grass – like a worn effigy over a grave where knight and hound have become mingled in monstrous ambiguity. The surface of the field is of the same wildness. It does not rise and fall in a few sea-like heavings, or in many little waves, nor is it level or in one long, gradual slope, but rising sleepily from west to east it is broken by sudden hollows and mounds. In one place the furze on a mound makes a little world for two or three pairs of linnets and whitethroats, and there are the largest and sweetest blackberries; there also a hundred young stems of brier spend spring and summer in perfecting the curves of their long leaps – curves that are like the gush of water over a dam, and yet crossing in multitudes without crowding, in all ways without discord, like the paths of the flight of swallows when they embroider the twilight air. In another place it is always marshy, the home of marigold and reed. One corner used to be dominated by a tall tented oak, of so majestic balance that when sawn through it stood long in the wind; there the pheasants are proud among bugle or centaury flowers. Here and there a smooth boulder protrudes, guarded by hundreds of blue scabious flowers which welcome butterflies of their own hue, and sometimes a peacock butterfly displays himself on the naked stone.

At the eastern and higher end the field becomes so narrow that it is like a lane, through which the hunt gloriously decants itself among the knolls. It is narrowed still more by a small pond, and round that a tall holly of solid shadow with glancing edges, an oak, an over-hanging thicket of bramble and thorn and three old butts of ash, where the fairy gold of toadstools is scattered abundantly, as if sown by one sweep of a generous hand. The pond is the home of one moorhen, which is always either swimming there or hastening to it from the field. It is but as large as a farmhouse kitchen, and yet the moorhen will not desert it, finding the caves among the roots as pleasing as attics to a boy; content with her seeming security though the road passes just above, and rich in her share of sun and moon and stars. To see the moorhen swimming in the narrow pond on a silent and misty autumn morning is to think, now with joy, now with pain, of solitude, but always with a reverie at last that is entangled among the dim, late stars – she possessing the solitary pond, in the solitary autumn country on a planet that is but an element in the solitude of the infinite; and her liquid hoot dwells long in the brain.

It is worth while to watch the pool at dawn, because, though it might seem to be but one of the myriad waters that light candles of adoration and celebration to every dawn, it has then the air, as the mist drips and tingles at the edge, of being a grey priest who has not yet done serving other gods than the dawn, and, until it puts on its white robes and glimmers altogether, it makes with the oak tree a group of pathetic revolt against the day – the oak might be a Saturn or a Lear, the pool in its gradual surrender to the light a Druid sheltering dear and unprosperous mysteries yet a little longer from the proud sun. Then the thrush sings on the holly crest with such blitheness as cannot, nevertheless, excel the water's glory in the fully risen light.

But whatever conversion the little pond undergoes on dawn after dawn, the field as a whole retains the same antiquity, which it announces so powerfully that I knew it on first crossing the stile. Perhaps the lawless shape of the field, its unusual undulations, its unkemptness in the midst of a land all rich with crops – perhaps these things suggested antiquity; but I think not – at least they do not explain it, for it was then strange, and now with all its familiarity it has rather gained than lost its power. It is the same when its outlines are concealed by mist and all I can see is the clover rough with silver dew, white mushrooms, and perhaps one red yolk of maple in the hollow air, and when the snow covers all but the myriad thistles blossoming with blue tits. Enter it in spring – the linnets sprinkle a song like audible sunlight – and yet the field is old. But November is its notable month. Its trees are all oaks and they have hardly lost a leaf; the leaves are falling continually from those smouldering sunset clouds of foliage, which, kingly rich, look as if they would never be poor. One skylark sings high over the field in the rainy sky. The blue rooks unsheathe themselves heavily from the branches and shine silverly and caw with genial voices. A pheasant explodes from a grass tussock underfoot. The air smells like the musky white wild rose; coming from the west it blows gently, laden with all the brown and golden savours of Wales and Devon and Wiltshire and Surrey which I know, and the scent lifts the upper lip so that you snuff deeply as a dog snuffs. A stoat goes with uplifted tail across the field. But the field itself – was there a great house here once and is it dead and yet vocal? Are its undulations and rude edges all that remain of an old wood? Or was there a battle here, and is the turf alive with death? Certainly there is death somewhere speaking eloquently to mortal men. It is not alive, but it laments something, and where there is sorrow there is life.

For just one day in September the goldfinches come and twitter, and are happy among the thistles, and fly away.

9. The Brook

The brook rises in a clear, grey, trembling basin at the foot of a chalk hill, among flowers of lotus and thyme and eyebright and rest-harrow. Here the stone curlew drinks, and above is the gently rounded encampment, ancient, and yet still young compared with the dusky spring which has something gnomish and earthy about it, though it takes the sun. It drops in thin, bright links over the chalk, and then for a time loses its way in playing with cresses and marsh marigolds, spreading out so finely that hardly will the ladybird drown that falls therein – falling at length in a cascade from one dead leaf to another down a hedge bank. Below, it nourishes the first forget-me-nots, by a gateway where it slips across the lane, and is dew-fed by the vetches and clovers that swaddle the posts of the gate. Now it is unheard and unseen in the darkness underneath dog's-mercury leaves until it has gained its first treble voice as, pausing by an interrupting branch, it fills a hollow and pours over in icy fingers to the ditch beneath. Here it has cuckoo-flowers and creeping jenny and butterbur to feed; thrushes drink of it; beetles dart across it like scullers that dream now and then upon their sculls. It learns now to sway the cress, to bow the brooklime, to brighten the sides of the minnows; the fledgeling of the robin that falls into it dies. It floats the catkin down, and out of it rises the azure dragon-fly. Sometimes it muffles its going in moss, but in a little while it gushes through drains and falls and falls with a now unceasing noise in a land where all the hollows are full of apple trees, rough grey with dewy clover, and through all the hollows winds the brook, dappled by blossom, leaned over by the bee-cradling, sleepy, meadow cranesbill flower; in its green bed the water-voles wear their submerged pathways. Now men have laid a slab of elm or of rude stone across it, and from those they lean to drink at haymaking or harvest; the children float on it pinnaces of bent reed, or set it to turn water-wheels of ash bark, or dip their cans in it for curving minnow or twisting tadpole or the little black circlers that meet and divide and pursue for a few April days. Already it has ranged along its margin rough, leaning willows garlanded by purple ivy; and their leaves that dip to the surface it will never allow to rest. The briers still overleap it in their long dreaming curves. The kingfisher sits over it and the small trout nestle in its bed. It enters many an ash copse and fills it with willow herb and meadow-sweet and all juicy plants, figwort and iris and orchis and hyacinth and reed, with osiers and their mists of crimson and gold. Nymph-like the brook brightens and curves its crystal flesh and waves its emerald hair under the bridges at field corners, where the brambles dip their blossoms, and the nightingale sings and the sedge warbler has its nest. For it the lonely willows in the flat fields shed their yellow leaves most pensively, like maidens casting their bridal garlands off. Three flowering apple trees in one islanded angle on a lawn of perfect grass, a most dream-worthy place, fit for the footprints of the beautiful,

White lope, blithe Helen, and the rest,

seem all its own; for there it first makes a deep sound in falling over a ledge among its own curded, quivering, and moonlit yellow foam. Thereafter it opens wide between broad low banks from which the cattle can step and stand among the reeds under serene tall ashes, and the lily petals float upon it that catch against the branches and against the hearts of men in distant towns. There, too, among the lilies the brook first takes the stars into its heart, but gaily with all its flowers and thick herbage and its rippling fall never still amidst the arrow-headed reed. It moves like the high autumn wain, followed by many children, who have time to leave it and gather flowers and are yet never left behind. The heron comes to it at dawn, knowing from afar the dark pool where it curves under a steep bank and grim oak roots, and slopes down to it solemn and eager and alone in the winter morning. The sand-martin and wagtail often pause in their flight and hover above the placid water and the cool, reflected reeds and water-mint. Where it is all of one depth, between straight banks of cowslip, the boys sit and let their feet waver in the flood and then roll or plunge in, with shouts and gurgling talk, while in the reeds, the dabchick waits with head just above water, trembling for her eggs or cheeping young. On Sunday the country lover, cruel all the week, brings his maid to the brook, and, suddenly tender and a little proud, shows her the moist, weed-covered nest and delights in her melting eyes. Fed now by other brooks, from its own hills and from little woodland springs, the brook consents to spread into a pool in an old garden, and in the sweet imprisonment of lily and rose and iris and oleander lies as if asleep, an indolent Leda contented with the white swan, and yet escaping all the time, its wild soul rejoicing yonder beneath the heavily overhanging honeysuckled thorns of the wide meadows again. Under the white highway the brook runs and lures men to lean from the parapet by the milestone and look at the water and take up some coolness and some bitterness from it when they return to the blinding miles. Its course is marked by alders and willows, shaping cornfield and pasture in divine meanders that seem to have learnt rather to be contented with travelling than to be eager for the goal. Could a man but wander in that way once more, like the child in the field of flowers so multitudinous that she did not know what to do, but closed her eyes and was happy yet! Now the otter plays there, and where the ash roots twist into many a cave. Through leagues of country the brook runs, passing high, silent woods and misty, hot, luxuriant, flowering thickets and wet, cloudy copses full at evening of confused birds' singing, which no one sees except the brook and the milk-white heifer who crowns herself in white roses in the shade as she stands in tall, moist, sumptuous angelica and watches her crowned image looking out of that fair sky in purest waters; then, suddenly emerging from this lonely country, it falls into a river and is lost or seems to be lost in the turbid, serious flow that is soon to know the sea.

10. *The Walnut Tree*

The immense, solitary, half-veiled autumn land is hissing with the kisses of rain in elms and hedgerows and grass, and underfoot the tunnelled soil gurgles and croaks. Secret and content, as if enjoying a blessed interval of life, are the small reedy pools where the moorhens hoot and nod in the grey water; beautiful the hundred pewits rising in ordered flight as they bereave the grey field and, wheeling over the leagues that seem all their own, presently make another field all a-flower by their alighting; almost happy once more is the tall, weedy mill by the broken water-gates, dying because no man inhabits it, its smooth wooden wheels and shoots and pillars fair and clean still under the red roof, though the wall is half fallen.

And in the heart of this, set in the dense rain, is a farmhouse far from any road; and round it the fields meet with many angles, and the hedges wind to make way, here, for a pond, deep underneath alders; there, for some scattered parcels of hayricks, on a grassy plot, encircling a large walnut tree; and for another pond, beside an apple orchard, whose trunks are lean and old and bent like the ribs of a wreck. A quadrangle of stalls, red tiled, of grey timber – trampled straw in their midst – adjoins the house, which is a red-grey cube, white-windowed, with tall, stout chimneys and steep, auburn roof, and green stonecrop frothing over its porch. In and out goes a rutted, grassy track, lined by decapitated and still-living remains of many ancient elms.

In the overhanging elm branches flicker the straws of the long-past harvest, and the spirits of summers and autumns long past cling to grass and ponds and trees.

The walnut tree among the ricks is dead. Against its craggy bole rest the shafts of a noble, blue wagon that seems coeval with it; long ladders are thrust up among its branches; deep in the brittle herbage underneath it lean or lie broken wheels, a rude wooden roller, the lovely timber of an antique plough, a knotted and rusted chain harrow, and the vast wooden wedge of the snow-plough that cleared the roads when winters were still grim. In the soft, straight rain these things are a buried world, the skeletons of a fair-seeming old life mingled with a sort of pleasant tranquillity as on the calm dim floor of a perilous main.

Half of the fruit trees are dead, save for their lichen and moss and their nests in fork and niche and the robin musing in the branches.

The duck pond, deep below, is all in shadow. The alders lean over it. Some have fallen, and the moor-hens have built on them, and the round vole sits there or drops off with the suddenness of fruit; but he cannot dive, for a million dead leaves are sunk or floating in the purple shadows.

Over all is the stillness of after harvest. Long ago the gleaners went home under the frosty moon, and the last wain left its memorial wisps in the elms. The rain possesses all, and a strange, funereal evocation calls up the bronzed corn again, and the heavy wagon and the grim, knitted chests of the bowing horses as they reach the bright-fruited walnut tree. The children laugh and run – who remember it in the workhouse now – and in a corner of the field the reaper slashes hatefully at the last standing rows. The harvest-queen sits on the topmost sheaves. They dance in the barn. Their voices are blithe and sweet; for the rain has washed away their flesh and quieted them now and recalls only golden hours, which linger in this idle autumn place and do not die but only hide themselves, as sunlight hides itself in yellow apples, in red roses, in crystal water, in a woman's eyes.

11. *The Village*

I

The village stands round a triangular, flat green that has delicate sycamores here and there at one side; beneath them spotted cows, or horses, or a family of tramps; and among them the swallows waver. On two sides the houses are close together. The third, beyond the sycamores, is filled by a green hedge, and beyond it an apple orchard on a gentle hill, and in the midst of that a farmhouse and farm-buildings so happily arranged that they look like a tribe of quiet monsters that have crawled out of the sandy soil to sun themselves. There the green woodpecker leaps and laughs in flight. Down each side of the green run yellow roads that cross one another at the angles, two going north, two going south, and one each to the east and west. Along these roads, for a little way, stand isolated cottages, most of them more ancient and odd than those in the heart of the village, as if they had some vagrant blood and could not stay in the neat and tranquil community about the green. Thus, one is built high above the road and is reached by a railed flight of stone steps. The roof of another slopes right to the ground on one side in a long curve, mounded by stonecrop and moss, out of which an elder tree is beginning to grow; and it has a crumbling tiled porch, like an oyster shell in colour and shape. One has a blank wall facing the road, and into the mortar of it, while it was yet fresh, the workmen have stuck fragments and even complete rounds of old blue and white saucers and plates. In others the mortar is decorated by two strokes of the trowel forming a wedge such as is found on old urns. In the ruinous orchard by a fourth, among nettles and buttercups, there is always a gipsy tent and white linen like blossom on the hedge. One of these houses seems to have strayed on to the green. Years ago someone pitched a tent there, and in course of time put an apple pip into the ground close by and watched it grow. The codling tree is now but a stump, standing at the doorway of a black wooden cottage named after it. Between it and the village pond go the white geese with heads in air.

Off one of those roads the church lifts a dark tower along with four bright ash trees out of a graveyard and meadow which are all buttercups. On three of the others there are plain, square, plastered inns, 'The Chequers,' 'The Black Horse,' 'The Four Elms,' where tramps sit on benches outside, and within the gamekeepers or passing carters sit and wear a little deeper the high curved arm-rests of the settles. But the chief inns stand opposite one another at one corner of the green, 'The Windmill,' and 'The Rose,' both of them rosy, half-timbered houses with sign-boards; the one beneath a tall, rocky-based elm which a wood-pigeon loves, the other behind a row of straight, pollarded limes; and opposite them is a pond on the edge of the green. In these inns the wayfarer drinks under the dark seventeenth-century beams; the worn pewter rings almost like glass; moss and ivy and lichen, and flowers in the windows, and human beings with laughter and talk and sighs at parting, decorate the ancient walls. The lime trees run in a line along the whole of one side of the green, and at their feet still creeps a stream where minnows hover and dart, and the black and white wagtail runs. Behind the trees are half the cottages of the village, some isolated among their bean rows and sunflowers, some attached in fantastic unions. Most are of one story, in brick, which the autumn creepers melt into, or in timber and tiles perilously bound together by old ivy; in one the Jacobean windows hint at the manor house of which other memory is gone; all are tiled. Their windows are white-curtained, with geranium or fuchsia or suspended campanula, or full of sweets, and onions, and rope, and tin tankards, and ham, and carrot-shaped tops, dimly seen behind leaded panes. Between the houses and the limes, the gardens are given up to flowers and a path, or they have a row of beehives: in one flower-bed the fragment of a Norman pillar rests quietly among sweet-rocket flowers. Instead of flower gardens, the wheelwright and the blacksmith have wagons, wheels, timber, harrows, coulters, spades, tyres, or fragments, heaped like wreckage on the sea floor, but with fowls and children or a robin amongst them, and perhaps, leaning against the trees, a brave, new wagon painted yellow and red or all blue.

On the other populous side of the green the houses are of the same family, without the limes; except that far back, among its lilac and humming maple foliage and flower, is the vicarage, a red, eighteenth-century house with long, cool, open windows, and a brightness of linen and silver within or the dark glimmer of furniture, and a seldom disturbed dream of lives therein leading 'melodious days.' Of how many lives the house has voicelessly chronicled the days and nights. It is aware of birth, marriage, death; into the wall is kneaded a record more pleasing than brass. With what meanings the vesperal sunlight slips through the narrow staircase window in autumn, making the witness pause. The moon has an expression proper to the dwellers there alone, nested among the limes or heaving an ivory shoulder above the tower of the church.

From one side to the other the straight starlings fly.

Along the roads go wagons and carts of faggots, or dung, or mangolds in winter; of oak bark in spring; of hay or corn in summer; of fruit or furniture in autumn.

A red calf, with white hind legs and white socks on her forelegs, strays browsing at the edge of the road. A close flock of sheep surges out of the dust and covers the green.

II

We were twelve in the tap of 'The Four Elms.' Five tramps were on one side; on the other, six pure-blooded labourers who had never seen London, and a seventh. A faggot was burning in the hearth, more for the sake of its joyful sound and perfume than for its heat. The sanded floor, cool and bright, received continually the red hollowed petals that bled from a rose on the table. The pewter glimmered; the ale wedded and unwedded innumerable shades of red and gold as it wavered in the mystic heart of the tankard. The window was held fast, shut by the stems of a Gloire de Dijon rose in bloom, and through it could be seen the gloom of an ocean of ponderous, heaving clouds, with a varying cleft of light between them and the hills which darkened the woods and made the wheat fields luminous.

Now and then a labourer extended his arm, grasped the tankard, slowly bent his arm whilst watching a gleam on the metal, and silently drank, his eyes lifted as if in prayer; then slowly put it back and saw a fresh circle being formed around it by the ale that was spilled.

The tramps leaned on a walnut table, as old as the house, polished so that it seemed to be coated with ice, here and there blackened with the heat transferred to it by a glass bottle standing in the sun. They looked at one another, changed their attitudes and their drinks, gesticulated, argued, swore, and sang. They became silent only when one of their number hammered a tune out of the reluctant piano. They were of several ages and types, of three nationalities, and had different manners and accents. One was a little epicurean Spanish skeleton who loved three things, his own pointed beard, a pot of cider, and the saying of Sancho Panza: 'I care more for the little black of the nail of my soul than my whole body.' He was a grasshopper in the fields of religion, scandal, and politics, and wore his hat scrupulously on one side. Another was a big, gentle Frenchman, with heavy eyelids, but a fresh boy's laugh. Early in the evening he scourged the republic; later, he laughed at the monarchy, the consulate, and the empire; and as he went to sleep touched his hat and whispered 'Vive la France!' His neighbour was fat, and repeated the Spaniard's remarks when they had been forgotten. It was to be wondered when he walked, what purpose his legs were made to serve. At the inn it was to be seen that they were a necessary addition to the four legs of a chair. He wanted nothing but a seat and not often wanted that. He was, I may say, made to be a sitting rather than a sapient animal, and had been lavishly favoured by Nature with that intention. The fourth, a pale, sour anarchist, hardly ever spoke, but was apparently an honest man, whom his indignant fellows called 'parson.' The last was one that had been born a poet, but never made one. He sang when he was asked, and later when he was asked not to sing; very quietly and very bitterly he cried when he had sung, indulging in a debauch of despair. Before we parted, the twelfth man sang all the sixteen verses of 'Sir Hugh of Lincoln,' in the hope of quenching their love of interminable songs. 'Heaven and Hell!' said the tramp, 'ye make me feel as if I was like Sir Hugh and Lady Helen and the Jew's daughter all in one. Curse ye I bless ye!'

Half-way through the evening the tramps were asleep. The labourers were as they were at the beginning. They sat arow according to age, and nothing but age distinguished them. Their opinions were those of the year in which they were born; for they were of that great family which, at the prime of life or earlier, seems to begin growing backwards, to quote 'grandfather' more often, and thus to give the observer a glimpse of the Dark Ages. Life to them was at once as plain and as inexplicable as the patterns on their willow cups or toby jugs. The eldest had a gift of dumbness that sometimes lasted nearly half a century, but once set going and wandering from ploughs to horses, and from horses to the king, his loyalty brought this forth:

'If that Edward wasn't king he ought to be.' Advancing to the subject of hay with a digression on the church, 'Which,' said the youngest, 'which came first, parson or hay?'

'What,' said the eldest in a short speech that occupied an hour of time, without interruption from the rest, who drank through his periods and sat watching him while he drank in the intervals by way of semi-colon. 'What is church for but rector to pray in? The parson prays for – for a good season, and a good season means a good hayrick like a church; well, then, Robert, George, Henry, and Palmston, I say that the day after they first wanted a rick they put up a church and put rector in to pray. I,' continued he, growing confident, 'remember the Crimea. I had but four boys then, but bad times they were. But we had tea, we had tea; the wife used to grate up toast and pour boiling water on it.'

'We called that coffee,' said the youngest, a lover of truth.

As the evening darkened and pipes went out and the scent of carnations came in with the wind, their speech became slower, with long intervals, as if they spoke only after ploughing a furrow. One by one they seemed to go out like the candles overhead, were silent, but never slept. The oldest, reddest and roundest of face, with white hair, looked like the sun at a mountain crest. The next seemed to be the spirit of beneficent rain, pale, vague, with moist eyes and tangled grey beard. The third was as the south wind, mild, cheerful, pink-faced, with a great rose in his button-hole. The fourth was the west wind, that lifts the hay from the level fields into clouds at a breath, that robs the harebell of its dew and stores it with rain – a mighty man with head on breast, and small hands united, and flowing hair. And the youngest was the harvest moon, glowing, with close hair and elusive features, a presence as he sat there rather than a man. So they were in the twilight, like a frieze on the white wall.

'Well, us have had fun, haven't us, George?' said the harvest moon. He received no answer as we passed out of 'The Four Elms,' for all but he had left the world where words are spoken and opinions held; and the hazel lane seemed to be a temple of the mysterious elements that make the harvest and the apple crop and the glory of the hops.

III

Walking in a country churchyard it is often hard to think of it as a place of death. The children play among the tombs. At Easter the village girls bring hither primroses from the woods, planting some, scattering others. Labourers meet and talk there, for the footpaths all converge towards the church. Lovers walk there. The grave-digger is indeed often busy there, but you may go many times and not find him at a grave, and it is seldom but he is planting flowers, pruning bushes, or mowing grass. On the tombs themselves, in epitaph or in lack of epitaph, is written the corporate wisdom of the village, its philosophy and its history half transmuted into poetry. Fancy can never be quiet as the eye, passes from Mary to Rebecca, from John to David, whose record let no one interpret untenderly. I have seen on an afternoon many a novel that shall never be written save as it is written here, deep without gloom, bitter without scandal, on those tablets that have kept their legends too long to be altogether fair. Even the harshest brevity has its fitness, as if it were penned by the right hand of Fate. And here, as in some other matters, we have made an insignificant advance upon our ancestors. The chief records of early races are their tombs. We know not so much that they lived as that they are dead. We guess at their lives from their dead bones. A tool, a weapon, a trinket, a favourite beast, is buried with them, conferring a life in death. In some ancient graves the bodies are found in a sitting posture, and if conjecture be just, we may suppose that the dead man once slept thus and dreamed, daring not to lie down, because no clothes kept off the frost or rain. So the endeavour to provide for an after life by utensils and food has not been wholly in vain. But 'Tombs,' said the poet, 'have their life and death.' The headstone is heir to the deceased and out in the world seeks a fortune, which is commonly bad. The fates of tombs have seldom been traced. The history of the epitaph has never been written. Thus is much common philosophy hidden away. Probably no body of literature could be found that is more fertile in homely truth and fancy. But collections of epitaphs either have no plan, or are intended to show only, what is curious, brilliant, or very old.

In this little churchyard a chapter or two of history and progress is easily seen. At the middle of the eighteenth century the sexton wrote the epitaphs, dealing out eulogy and fact with a generous hand. After him came a series of nonentities, whose epitaphs are as like one another as Windsor chairs. Honest regret, or 'smiling through tears,' was ousted by complacent joy at the celestial lot of the deceased. Decent friendship was replaced by encomiastic fraud. Like all fashions it was feeble, but like all fashions it had some good; it produced models of accurate expression of 'not what he was, but what he should have been.' Then in the nineteenth century followed a silent age. 'He was alive, and is dead'; tombstones with such inscriptions are like men who do not speak in company, and unlike them, they never disappoint. They say, at any rate, not more than is written of honest men in heaven. The children of those silent people did little but irrelevantly quote or para-phrase the Bible and Dr. Watts. The epitaphs were now thought worthy of a clear, large type; the fashion at least taught the children to spell. Some there were who gained no small village reputation by a diligent study of these sentences. Even the wiser pillars of the village, whether they could read or not, were sure of awe and admiration among their audience, if their speeches – political,

religious, or scandalous – were launched by 'As the great
Dr. Watts wrote . . .' or 'In the words of Amos, whom
you may know . . .' Not of this period, but first notorious
then, was the epitaph on Sir –, Bart. His family being
still one of splendour and influence, everything connected with it was held in esteem. It was, therefore, not
unnatural that the admirers of an aged spinster should
put upon her tomb the epitaph that was picked out with
letters of gold on that of the young baronet:

> The good die young.

Strangers are apt to wonder first at the longevity
common in the parish – then at the humour of the thing
– and go away both contented and deceived. For some
time it was not uncommon to quote a grave passage
from Shakespeare, with decent omission of the author's
name; when, however, a revolutionist not only published 'Shakespeare' on a headstone, but 'Romeo and
Juliet' too, the vicar was approached, the sexton ran a
risk every day, the innkeeper, the J.P. was approached.
The bereaved person had in the meantime erased the
offending words, and until recently you might read:

> God rest his soul! He was a merry man,

beneath which the curious eye may still discover 'Kings
iii,' placed there in homage to parish prejudice. The
storm almost raised by the introduction of two lines by
Robert Burns – 'a poet as well as a drunkard,' according
to village rumour – is still remembered. The parish clerk

having doubted whether it was in 'Ancient and Modern,' took refuge in the book of Ecclesiastes, until a confidant (a fearless thinker and a friend of Chartists) swore it was written by a lord. The vicar was questioned. Opening a book whose cover was well known to the doubter, and repeating with nasal unction the offending words, he drew tears and apologies from the man. After that comparative freedom of choice was enjoyed, and some went bravely back to

> Afflictions sore long years I bore,

as recently as 1885. Tennyson was in favour at that time; no one grumbled since he was the author of

> That good man, the clergyman.

But when I brush aside the leaves and flowers of herb honesty, growing by the older graves, although I am willing to admit that the village view of death has become more solemn, I cannot but wish back again the author of

> This world has lost old John the sexton,
> What business has he in the next one?

Where are the robuster views of which this is a late reminder? The gay, the fanciful, the calmly elaborate epitaphs seem to have gone for ever, and in the newer portion of the churchyard it is hard not to think of death, unless we turn to the unnamed little mounds that rise and fall like summer waters, so calm, so soft, so green, that fancy cannot make them aught save pillows for the weary. I have seen a tramp sleeping there and envied him his unconscious return to the good old insouciance which was warm with the thought that in the midst of death we are yet alive.

IV

From the churchyard run twelve footpaths; some ending at farmhouses close by; some losing themselves in the nearest road; one leading nowhere, nor of any use to-day, since the house which drew it thither across the wheat is under the cow-parsley and grass; one going on without end, touching here and there a farmhouse, crossing a road, passing in at the door of an inn and out through the garden, as if some friendly man had made the path by following his heart's desire. Most of the paths lead up on to the hills among which the village is set. From the highest part, in spring, the warmth and life of the scene below contrast strangely with its immense age, as the new brazen leaves of the oak with their ancient trunk. The houses are old, the church older, the farm wall yonder is partly the remains of a castle of Norman date. The hedges twist so fantastically because they also are old, marking ancient paths, the edges of departed woods, the gradually advancing line of men's camp-fires overcoming the wilderness. In that hollow the gemote used to sit. Here a company of cavalry charged down the hill and to a man went over the chalk pit to the road and to death. There stood an abbey, now speaking only through a curve added to the undulations of the land. In the next village a poet was born. A dolmen rises out of the wheat in one field, like a quotation from an unknown language in the fair page of a book. The names of the places are in the same language, and yet how smoothly they issue from the lips. The little roads, so old, wind among the fields timidly, as if they marked the path of one creeping with difficulty through forest coeval with the world. Some roads have disappeared – there where the wheat grows thin in a narrow band across the field. Another is disappearing; worn to the depth of some feet below the surrounding fields by the feet of adventurers, lovers, exiles, plain endurers of life, its end is to become a groove full of hazels and birds, the innermost kernel of the land, because nobody owns and nobody uses it. In contrast with those, how certain of its aim the great road running east and west, the road of conqueror, pilgrim, merchant, the embodiment of will and opportunity; and that, too, so old that heron and rook seem to recognize it as they go over at nightfall. There is no age that does not play its part in the symphony of this June scene. And yet, standing still upon the ridge commanding it, when the roads are overhung by the blithe new green of beech leaves and paved with their ruddy chaff, these things become a part of the silence and clear air which they trouble and enrich as do the storied pavements and walls of a cathedral, thrilling the ear and shaming the powers of the eye, so that in the end the mind vibrates with the strangely interwoven melodies of joy in the life that still triumphs within us, and of acquiescence in the death which will leave of us not so much trace as can add to the silence and clear air one tone audible to mortal men.

12. A Winter Morning

Night was soon to pass into a winter day as I looked out of the window to see what kind of a world it was that had been, since I began to read, shutting me off effectually from everything but my book.

> And but the flitter-winged verse must tell,
> For truth's sake, what woe afterwards befel,
> 'Twould humour many a heart to leave them thus,
> Shut from the busy world of more incredulous.

The words were still fresh in my brain.

But, outside, the trees and barns and shed were quiet and dim, and as much submerged and hidden from the air in which I had been living as the green streets of motionless lily and weed at the bottom of some lonely pool where carp and tench go slowly. The road went straight away from the window to the invisible beyond; hard and dry, it was trying to shine, as if it recalled the sunlight. Half-way along, at one side, under a broad oak, there was a formless but pregnant shadow. The farm-buildings that lay about the road were huddled, dark, colourless, and indistinguishable because of their shadows; they might have been heaped up by a great plough, of which the road was the shining furrow; they were not so much the vague wreckage of what I had known yesterday, as a chaos out of which, perhaps, something was to be born. Yet the outside world was vaster than it had seemed when I could see three ranges of hills and guess at the sea beyond; and strange it was when the words –

> She saw the young Corinthian Lycius
> Charioting foremost in the envious race
> Like a young love, with calm, uneager face,
> And fell into a swooning love of him –

came back to me. How frail and perilous and small was the poet's shielded world! The outside world threatened it as the smooth escarpment of tall, toppling water threatens the little piping sea-bird. And yet this poet's world was for the time being my life. Beyond his words there were, perhaps, the gay, the dear, the beautiful persons whom I knew; Nobby, the tinker, and many more; but probably they slept; they were vain if they were not fictitious; if they could be supposed to live, my only proof of it was that somehow they were connected with a very distant light that refused to go out among the westward copses. They were hardly more credible than the words of a stale preacher talking of charity, or an artful poet writing of love.

So I clung to Keats, the reality, until the road grew almost white, and under that broad oak some rational, nay, beautiful outlines began to appear, which the shadow enveloped like a cocoon. The outlines were hardly built until they were seen to be a wagon, and its birth out of the shadow was a mighty thing that shared the idiom of stately trees and the motions of great waters and of cliffs that look on sunset and a noble sea. Dimly, uncertainly, powerfully, never quite expressing itself in any known language – as was natural in what seemed to belong to an early brood of the giant earth – the wagon emerged, with ponderous wheels and slender, curving timbers and trailing shafts. The chariot of Dis coming up to Persephone looked thus majestic. Yet the wagon suggested nothing definite, at least no history. It had no such articulate power. But antiquity played about it as, an hour before, it had played about my shelves and books. It was simply the richer for its long life, like a violin or a wise man; and, like them, it neither carried its legend on its exterior nor encouraged anything more than joyful surmise.

It was the one cleary visible piece of man's work among all those potent shadows and uncertain forms of roof and wall; it was crowned by the last stars. Becoming clearer as morning came, it was an important part of the re-creation of the world, and involved in it, just as a brazen image may seem to be part of the good fortune or calamity which follows prayer to it. It filled the white road with emotion. It was more intelligible than some men are when they say 'I worship' or 'I love.' Keats left my mind. From my memory, I added melodies of voice and harp and reed, and noise of seas and winds in forests and houses by night, and organ music, with its many demons blithe and terrible, exploring the skyey roof of some cathedral and knocking at the clerestory to get out, floating, sad or happy, about the aisles, and settling at last to make the old purples and greens and blues in the glass more solemn than before; and yet I could not reproduce the melody or anything like it, with which the old wagon pervaded the farmyard. Slowly the light came, and the world was filled with it as imperceptibly as the brain with a great thought. It fell upon the spokes of the wagon wheel, and they seemed to move. Then all was over.

The clear face of things which it is so hard to enjoy was back again. The determined starlings flew swift and straight overhead. The clouds about the risen sun went stately upon their errands through the sky.

13. Under the Moor

It was June, but it had been like March for many miles upon the rough moor until, with the dawn, I came to a lowland where there were mossy fields with clear rain pools among the flowering gorse; and meadows cut into two planes by small, perpendicular cliffs of stone, so that on one the cattle were already feeding in the early light and on the other still lying down; and wheat fields that had islands of stone in their midst; and then at last an immense meadow sloping down towards fresh oak woods and the sea, and rising out of it rounded beechen knolls which, Druid-like, preserved the night under their domes of foliage, though all the grass was flooded by the slow tides of dawn. The white cow-parsley flowers hovered around me on invisible stems and gave out the thick summer flavours of nettles and myriad grasses. And lying down and sleeping in the sun until morning was hot, I awoke and seemed to hear a tale of the south as the air grew mazy with the scent of elder and thyme and the colour of bird's-foot lotus and all the grass, and the sky leaned down upon the earth in milky purples. It was just such a change from the poor land to the rich as is expressed in the ancient tale of Cherry of Zennor told by Hunt in his *Popular Romances of the West of England*.

The girl, Cherry of Zennor, could not contentedly put

up with her life at home, because her parents were poor, living on potatoes and fish, and she, though she was pretty and could run like a hare, had never a ribbon for her curls nor a new frock to go to church or to fair in. So she set out to get a servant's place somewhere in the 'low countries.'

The road was long and she was homesick by the time she had reached a four-went way. There she sat down and cried, but had scarcely recovered when she saw a gentleman coming up to her. He bade her 'good morning,' and asked her whither she went; and when she said that she was off to look for a servant's place, he told her that he was in search of just such a clean and handsome girl for his own house. So Cherry went off with him, to milk his cow and look after his child; and she was to have good clothes when she got there.

They went down and down for a long way; the road was clouded over by trees and was growing darker and darker, when suddenly the man opened a gate in a wall and told her that there it was that he lived. She had never seen a garden so rich in fruit and flowers and singing birds. Was it enchanted? But no, the man was no fairy; he was too big. Presently his child appeared, a boy with piercing and crafty eyes, and an old hag, called 'Aunt Prudence,' who prepared a choice supper for the girl; and she ate of it heartily. Cherry slept with the child at the top of the house and was told that, even if she could not sleep, she was to keep her eyes shut up there and not to speak to the boy; at dawn she was to wash him at a spring in the garden and rub his eyes – never her own – with an ointment; then she was to milk the cow and give the boy a bowl of the last milk; she was at all times to avoid curiosity.

All this she did until it came to milking the cow. But Cherry saw no cow and was calling, 'Pruit! Pruit! Pruit!' when out she came from among the trees as if from nowhere. All day, but it was easy work, she scalded milk, made butter, cleaned platters and bowls with water and sand, picked the fruit, weeded the garden. Sometimes the man kissed her for her pains.

A year passed. Aunt Prudence was sent away because she took Cherry into one of the forbidden rooms, where the floor was like glass and it was full of people turned to stone. Sometimes the master went away and left Cherry alone with the child.

The ointment was still a puzzle – but surely it made the child's eyes see many things. So one day she anointed her own eyes with it. It burned her painfully, and running to the spring to wash it away she learned its power. For there, at the bottom of the water, was a world of little people at play and among them her master; and looking up she saw that the branches of the trees and the flowers and the grass were crowded with the same joyous people. Another day she looked through the keyhole of one of the forbidden rooms and saw her master there, and many ladies too, all singing, and one of these who looked like a queen he kissed. So when, as they were fruit gathering some time afterwards, the master leaned forward to kiss her, she struck him on the face, saying that he might kiss the small people under the water. Next morning very early he called her from her bed, led her by the light of a lantern up the dark lane for a long way, and then disappeared, after telling her that at times she would still be able to see him on the hills; and when she had recovered from her sorrow she went home.

14. June – Hampshire – The Golden Age – Traherne

Now day by day, indoors and out of doors, the conquest of spring proceeds to the music of the conquerors. One evening the first chafer comes to the lamp, and his booming makes the ears tremble with dim apprehension. He climbs, six-legged and slow, up the curtain, supporting himself now and then by unfurling his wings, or if not he falls with a drunken moan, then begins to climb again, and at last blunders about the room like a ball that must strike something, the white ceiling, the white paper, the lamp, and when he falls he rests. In his painful climbing he looks human, as perhaps a man looks angelic to an angel; but there is nothing lovelier and more surprising than the unfurling of his pinions like a magic wind-blown cloak out of that hard mail.

Another day the far-off woods in a hot, moist air first attain their rich velvet mossiness, and even near at hand the gorse-bushes all smouldering with bloom are like clouds settled on the earth, having no solidity, but just colour and warmth and pleasantness.

The broad-backed chestnuts bloom. On the old cart-lodge tiles the vast carapace of the house-leek is green and rosy, and out of the midst of it grow dandelions and grass, and the mass of black mould which it has accumulated in a century bends down the roof.

The hawthorn-bloom is past before we are sure that

it has reached its fulness. Day after day its warm and fragrant snow clouded the earth with light, and yet we waited, thinking surely to-morrow it will be fairer still, and it was, and the next day we thought the same and we were careless as in first love, and then one day it lay upon the grass, an empty shell, the vest of departed loveliness, and another year was over. The broad grass is full of buttercups' gold or it is sullen silvery under a burning afternoon sun, without wind, the horizon smoky, the blue sky and its white, still clouds almost veiled by heat; the red cattle are under the elms; the unrippled water slides under sullen silvery willows.

The night-haze peels off the hills and lets the sun in upon small tracts of wood – upon a group of walnuts in the bronze of their fine, small leaf – upon downland grass, and exposes blue sky and white cloud, but then returns and hides the land, except that the dewy ground-ash and the ivy and holly gleam; and two cuckoos go over crying and crying continually in the hollow vale.

Already the ash-keys hang in cool, thick bunches under the darker leaves. The chestnut-bloom is falling. The oak-apples are large and rosy. The wind is high, and the thunder is away somewhere behind the pink mountains in the southern sky or in the dark drifts overhead. And yet the blue of the massy hangers almost envelops the beechen green; the coombes and the beeches above and around their grassy slopes of juniper are soft and dim, and far withdrawn, and the nightjar's voice is heard as if the wind there were quiet. The rain will not come; the plunging wind in the trees has a sound of waterfalls all night, yet cannot trouble the sleep of the orange-tip butterfly on the leopard's-bane's dead flower.

Now the pine blooms in the sandy lands, above the dark-fronded brake and glaucous-fruited whortleberry, the foxgloves break into bell after bell under the oaks and birches. The yellow broom is flowering and scented, and the white lady's bedstraw sweetens the earth's breath. The careless variety of abundance and freshness makes every lane a bride. Suddenly, in the midst of the sand, deep meadows gleam, and the kingfisher paints the air with azure and emerald and rose above the massy water tumbling between aspens at the edge of a neat, shaven lawn, and, behind that, a white mill and miller's house with dark, alluring windows where no one stirs.

June puts bronze and crimson on many of her leaves. The maple-leaves and many of the leaves of thorn and bramble and dogwood are rosy; the hazel-leaves are rosy-brown; the herb-robert and parsley are rose-red; the leaves of ash and holly are dark lacquered. The copper beeches, opulently sombre under a faintly yellowed sky, seem to be the sacred trees of the thunder that broods above. Presently the colour of the threat is changed to blue, which soiled white clouds pervade until the whole sky is woolly white and grey and moving north. There is no wind, but there is a roar as of a hurricane in the trees far off; soon it is louder, in the trees not so remote; and in a minute the rain has traversed half a mile of woods, and the distant combined roar is swallowed up by the nearer pattering on roof and pane and leaf, the dance of leaves, the sway of branches, the trembling of whole trees under the flood. The rain falls straight upon the hard road, and each drop seems to leap upward from it barbed. Great drops dive among the motionless, dusty nettles. The thunder unloads its ponderous burden upon the resonant floor of the sky; but the sounds of the myriad leaves and grass-blades drinking all but drowns the boom, the splitting roar, and the echo in the hills. When it is over it has put a final sweetness into the blackbird's voice and into the calm of the evening garden when the voice of a singer does but lay another tribute at the feet of the enormous silence. Frail is that voice as the ghost-moth dancing above the grass so faithfully that it seems a flower attached to a swaying stem, or as the one nettle-leaf that flutters in a draught of the hedge like a signalling hand while all the rest of the leaves are as if they could not move again, or as the full moon that is foundering on a white surf in the infinite violet sky. More large and more calm and emptier of familiar things grows the land as I pass through it, under the hoverings of the low-flying but swiftly turning nightjar, until at midnight only a low white mist moves over the gentle desolation and warm silence. The mist wavers, and discloses a sky all strewn with white stars like the flowers of an immense jessamine. It closes up again, and day is born unawares in its pale arms, and earth is for the moment nothing but the tide of downs flowing west and the branch of red roses that hangs heavily laden and drowsed with its weight and beauty over my path, dipping its last spray in the dew of the grass.

The day is a Sunday, and no one is on foot or on wheel in the broad arable country that ripples in squares of green, or brown, or yellow, or grey, to the green

Downs and their dark, high-perched woods. As if for some invisible beholder, the green elders and their yellow-green flower-buds make their harmony with the yellow-lichened barns against which they lean; the grass and the noble trees, the groups of wayside aspen, the line of horse-chestnuts, the wych-elms on both sides of the road, the one delicate sycamore before the inn and the company of sycamores above the cross – the spacious thatch and tiles of the farmyard quadrangle – the day newly painted in white and blue – the green so green in the hedges, and the white and purple so pure in the flowers – all seem to be meant for eyes that know nothing of Time and of what 'brought death into the world and all our woe.' And in this solitude the young birds are very happy. They have taken possession of the thick hedges, of the roadside grass, of the roads themselves. They flutter and run and stumble there; they splash in the pools and in the dust, which not a wheel nor a foot has marked. These at least are admitted into the kingdom along with that strange wildfowl that lives 'to maintain the trade and mystery of typographers.'

Such a day, in the unblemished summer land, invariably calls up thoughts of the Golden Age. As mankind has looked back to a golden age, so the individual, repeating the history of the race, looks back and finds one in his own past. Historians and archaeologists have indeed made it difficult for men of our time to look far back for a golden age. We are shown a skull with supraciliary prominences and are told that its owner, though able to survive the mammoth by means of tools of flint, lived like the Tasmanian of modern times; and

his was no Golden Age. Then we look back to heroic
ages which poetry and other arts have magnified – to
the Greece of Homer or Pheidias, to the Ireland of
Cuchulain, to the Wales of Arthur, to the England which
built the great cathedrals or produced Chaucer, Sir Philip
Sidney, Izaak Walton.

In the same way, few men can now look back to their
childhood like Traherne and say that

All appeared new and strange at first, inexpressibly rare and
delightful and beautiful. I was a little stranger which at my
entrance into the world was saluted and surrounded with
innumerable joys. My knowledge was Divine. I knew by
intuition those things which since my Apostasy I collected
again by the highest reason. My very ignorance was advantage-
ous. I seemed as one brought into the Estate of Innocence. All
things were spotless and pure and glorious; yea, and infinitely
mine, and joyful and precious. I knew not that there were
any sins or complaints or laws. I dreamed not of poverties,
contentions, or vices. All tears and quarrels were hidden from
mine eyes. Everything was at rest, free and immortal. I knew
nothing of sickness or death or rents or exaction, either for
tribute or bread. . . . All Time was Eternity, and a perpetual
Sabbath. Is it not strange, that an infant should be heir of the
whole world and see those mysteries which the books of the
learned never unfold?

We blink, deliberately or not, unpleasant facts in our
own lives, as in the social life of Greece or the Middle
Ages. Some have no need to do so; robustly or sensitively
made, their childish surroundings have been such as to

meet their utmost needs or to draw out their finest powers or to leave them free. Ambition, introspection, remorse had not begun. The vastness and splendour and gloom of a world not understood, but seen in its effects and hardly at all in its processes, made a theatre for their happiness which – especially when seen through a mist of years – glorify it exceedingly, and it becomes like a ridge of the far-off downs transfigured in golden light, so that we in the valley sigh at the thought that where we have often trod is heaven now. Such beauties of the earth, seen at a distance and inaccessibly serene, always recall the equally inaccessible happiness of childhood. Why have we such a melting mood for what we cannot reach? Why, as we are whirled past them in a train, does the sight of a man and child walking quietly beside a reedy pond, the child stooping for a flower and its gossip unheard – why should we tremble to reflect that we have never tasted just that cloistered balm?

Perhaps the happiest childhoods are those which pass completely away and leave whole tracts of years without a memory; those which are remembered are fullest of keen joy as of keen pain, and it is such that we desire for ourselves if we are capable of conceiving such fantastic desires. I confess to remembering little joy, but to much drowsy pleasure in the mere act of memory. I watch the past as I have seen workless, homeless men leaning over a bridge to watch the labours of a titanic crane and strange workers below in the ship running to and fro and feeding the crane. I recall green fields, one or two whom I loved in them, and though no trace of such happiness as I had remains, the incorruptible tranquillity of it all breeds fancies of great happiness. I recall many scenes: a church and churchyard and black pigs running down from them towards me in a rocky lane – ladslove and tall, crimson, bitter dahlias in a garden – the sweetness of large, moist yellow apples eaten out of doors – children: I do not recall happiness in them, yet the moment that I return to them in fancy I am happy. Something like this is true also of much later self-conscious years. I cannot – I am not tempted to – allow what then spoiled the mingling of the elements of joy to reappear when I look back. The reason, perhaps, is that only an inmost true self that desires and is in harmony with joy can perform these long journeys, and when it has set out upon them it sheds those gross incrustations which were our curse before.

Many are the scenes thus to be recalled without spot or stain. It is a May morning, warm and slightly breezy after midnight rain. In the beech woods the trees are unloading the dew, which drops from leaf to leaf and down on to the lemon-tinged leaves of dark dog's mercury. At the edge of the wood the privet branches are bent down by the weight of raindrops of the size of peas. The dewy white stitchwort stars and the feathered grasses are curved over on the banks. The sainfoin is hoary and sparkling as I move. Already the sun is hot and the sky blue, with faint white clouds in whirls. And in the orchard-trees and drenched luxuriant hedges the garden-warbler sings a subdued note of rushing, bubbling liquidity as of some tiny brook that runs in quick pulsations among the fleshy-leaved water-plants. The bird's head is uplifted; its throat is throbbing; it moves restlessly from branch to branch, but always renews its song on the new perch; being leaf-like, it is not easily seen. And sometimes through this continuous jargon the small, wild song of the blackcap is heard, which is the utmost expression of moist warm dawns in May thickets of hawthorn-bloom and earliest roses. On such a dawn the very spirit bathes in the dew and nuzzles into the fragrance with delight; but it is no sooner left behind with May than it has developed within me into an hour and a scene of utmost grace and bliss, save that I am in it myself.

It is curious, too, how many different kinds of Eden or Golden Age Nature has in her gift, as if she silently recorded the backward dreams of each generation and reproduced them for us unexpectedly. It is, for instance, an early morning in July. The cows pour out from the milking-stalls and blot out the smell of dust with their breath in the white road between banks of hazel and thorn. The boy who is driving them to the morning's pasture calls to them monotonously, persuasively, in turn, as each is tempted to crop the roadside sward: 'Wo, Cherry! Now, Dolly! Wo, Fancy! Strawberry! . . . Blanche! . . . Blossom! . . . Cowslip! . . . Rosy! . . . Smut! . . . Come along, Handsome! . . . Wo, Snowdrop! . . . Lily! . . . Darky! . . . Roany! . . . Come along, Annie!' Here the road is pillowed with white aspen-down, there more fragrant than pines with the brown sheddings of yew, and here thick with the dry scent of nettle and cow-parsnip, or glorious in perfect mingling of harebell and foxglove among the bracken and popping gorse on the roadside. The cows turn into the aftermath of the sainfoin, and the long valley echoes to their lowing. After them, up the road, comes a gipsy-cart, and the boy hangs on the gate to see the men and women walking, black-haired, upright, bright-eyed, and on the name-board of the cart the words: 'Naomi Sherwood, Burley, Hampshire.' These things also propose to the roving, unhistoric mind an Eden, one still with us, one that is passing, not, let us hope, the very last.

Some of these scenes, whether often repeated or not, come to have a rich symbolical significance; they return persistently and, as it were, ceremoniously – on festal days – but meaning I know not what. For example, I never see the flowers and scarlet-stained foliage of herb-robert growing out of old stone-heaps by the way-side without a feeling of satisfaction not explained by a long memory of the contrast between the plant and the raw flint; so also with the drenched lilac-bloom leaning out over high walls of unknown gardens; and inland cliffs, covered with beech, jutting out westward into a bottomless valley in the mist of winter twilights, in silence and frost. Something in me belongs to these things, but I hardly think that the mere naming of them will mean anything except to those – many, perhaps – who have experienced the same. A great writer so uses the words of every day that they become a code of his own which the world is bound to learn and in the end take unto itself. But words are no longer symbols, and to say 'hill' or 'beech' is not to call up images of a hill or a beech-tree, since we have so long been in the habit of using the words for beautiful and mighty and noble things very much as a book-keeper uses figures without seeing gold and power. I can, therefore, only try to suggest what I mean by the significance of the plant in the stone-heap, the wet lilac, the misty cliff, by comparing it with that of scenes in books where we recognize some power beyond the particular and personal. All of Don Quixote's acts have this significance; so have the end of Mr Conrad's story of *Youth* and the opening of Mr Hudson's *El Ombu* – the old man sitting on a summer's day under the solitary tree to tell the history 'of a house that had been.' Malory's *Morte d'Arthur* is full of scenes like this. For ten centuries, from the battle of Badon to the writing of *Morte d'Arthur*, these stories were alive on the lips of many kinds of men and women in many lands, from Connemara to Calabria. Many of these men and women survive only in the turns which their passionate hearts gave to these ghostly, everlastingly wandering tales. Artists have worked upon them. Bards have sung them, and the sound of their harping is entangled in the words that have reached us to-day. This blending of many bloods is suggested by the Saracen in the *Morte d'Arthur* who was descended from Hector and Alexander and Joshua and Maccabæus; by Taliesin, whose 'original country is the region of the summer stars,' who was with Noah and Alexander and at the birth of Christ. And thus has the tale become so full in the ear of humanity, so rich in scenes designed to serve only an immediate purpose, yet destined by this grace to move all kinds of men in manifold ways. Such is the chess-playing in *The Dream of Rhonabwy*; the madness of Tristram when he ran naked in the woods many days, but was lured by the music of a damsel playing on his own harp; the speech of Arthur at the scattering of his knights in the Sangraal quest; Launcelot's fighting with the black knights against the white; Launcelot's adventures ending at the castle of Carbonek, where he put on all his arms and armour and went – 'and the moon shone clear' – between the lions at the gate and forced open the door and saw the 'Holy Vessel, covered with red samite, and many angels about it'; and Arthur and Guenevere watching the dead Elaine in the barge; and in the wars of Arthur and Launcelot, the scene opening with the words: 'Then it befell upon a day in harvest-time, Sir Launcelot looked over the walls, and spake on high unto King Arthur and Sir Gawaine. . . .'

No English writer has expressed as well as Traherne the spiritual glory of childhood, in which Wordsworth saw intimations of immortality. He speaks of 'that divine light wherewith I was born' and of his 'pure and virgin apprehensions,' and recommends his friend to pray earnestly for these gifts: 'They will make you angelical, and wholly celestial.' It was by the 'divine knowledge' that he saw all things in the peace of Eden:

The corn was orient and immortal wheat, which never should be reaped, nor was ever sown. I thought it had stood from everlasting to everlasting. The dust and stones of the street were as precious as gold; the gates were at first the end of the world. The green trees when I saw them first through one of the gates transported and ravished me; their sweetness and unusual beauty made my heart to leap and almost mad with ecstasy; they were such strange and wonderful things. The Men! O what venerable and reverend creatures did the aged seem! Immortal Cherubims! And young men glittering and sparkling angels, and maids strange seraphic pieces of life and beauty! Boys and girls tumbling in the street, and playing, were moving jewels. I knew not that they were born or should die; but all things abided eternally as they were in their proper places. Eternity was manifest in the light of the day, and something infinite behind everything appeared, which tallied with my expectation and moved my desire . . .

Yet was this light eclipsed. He was 'with much ado' perverted by the world, by the temptation of men and worldly things and by 'opinion and custom,' not any 'inward corruption or depravation of Nature.'

For he tells us how he once entered a noble dining-room and was there alone 'to see the gold and state and carved imagery,' but wearied of it because it was dead, and had no motion. A little afterwards he saw it 'full of lords and ladies and music and dancing,' and now pleasure took the place of tediousness, and he perceived, long after, that 'men and women are, when well understood, a principal part of our true felicity.' Once again, 'in a lowering and sad evening, being alone in the field, when all things were dead quiet,' he had the same weariness, nay, even horror. 'I was a weak and little child, and had forgotten there was a man alive in the earth.' Nevertheless, hope and expectation came to him and comforted him, and taught him 'that he was concerned in all the world.' That he was 'concerned in all the world' was the great source of comfort and joy which he found in life, and of that joy which his book pours out for us. Not only did he see that he was concerned in all the world, but that river and corn and herb and sand were so concerned. God, he says, 'knoweth infinite excellencies' in each of these things; 'He seeth how it relateth to angels and men.' In this he anticipated Blake's *Auguries of Innocence*. He seems to see the patterns which all living things are for ever weaving. He would have men strive after this divine knowledge of things and of their place in the universe.

He came to believe that 'all other creatures were such that God was Himself in their creation, that is, Almighty Power wholly exerted; and that every creature is indeed as it seemed in my infancy, not as it is commonly apprehended.'

Yet he feels the superiority of man's soul to the things which it apprehends: 'One soul in the immensity of its intelligence is greater and more excellent then the whole world.' Even so Richard Jefferies prayed that his soul 'might be more than the cosmos of life.' The soul is greater than the whole world because it is capable of apprehending the whole world, because it is spiritual, and the spiritual nature is infinite. Thus Traherne was led to the splendid error of making the sun 'a poor little dead thing.' Or perhaps it was a figure of speech used to convince the multitude of his estimation of man's soul as above all visible things. In the same spirit he speaks of 'this little Cottage of Heaven and Earth as too small a gift, though fair,' for beings of whom he says: 'Infinity we know and feel by our souls; and feel it so naturally, as if it were the very essence and being of the soul'; and again, with childlike simplicity and majesty:

'Man is a creature of such noble principles and severe

expectations, that could he perceive the least defect to be in the Deity, it would infinitely displease him.'

He could not well have thought of man except loftily, since he was himself one whom imagination never deserted – imagination the greatest power of the mind by which not poets only live and have their being:

'For God,' says he, 'hath made you able to create worlds in your own mind which are more precious unto Him than those which He created; and to give and offer up the world unto Him, which is very delightful in flowing from Him, but made more in returning to Him.'

That power to create worlds in the mind is the imagination, and is the proof that the creature liveth and is divine. 'Things unknown,' he says, 'have a secret influence on the soul,' and 'we love we know not what.' The spirit can fill the whole world and the stars be your jewels: 'You never enjoy the world aright, till the sea itself floweth in your veins, till you are clothed with the heavens, and crowned with the stars, and perceive yourself to be the sole heir of the whole world.' And our inheritance is more than the world, 'because men are in it who are every one sole heirs as well as you.' It is a social mysticism. 'The world,' he says in another place, 'does serve you, not only as it is the place and receptacle of all your joys, but as it is a great obligation laid upon all mankind, and upon every person in all ages, to love you as himself; as it also magnifieth all your companions.' His is the true 'public mind,' as he calls it. 'There is not,' he says in another place – 'there is not a man in the whole world that knows God, or himself, but he must honour you. Not only as an Angel or as a Cherubim, but as one redeemed by the blood of Christ, beloved by all Angels, Cherubims, and Men, the heir of the world, and as much greater than the Universe, as he that possesseth the house is greater than the house. O what a holy and blessed life would men lead, what joys and treasures would they be to each other, in what a sphere of excellency would every man move, how sublime and glorious would their estate be, how full of peace and quiet would the world be, yea, of joy and honour, order and beauty, did men perceive this of themselves, and had they this esteem for one another!'

Here, as in other passages, he seems to advance to the position of Whitman, whom some have blamed for making the word 'divine' of no value because he would apply it to all, whereas to do so is no more than to lay down that rule of veneration for men – and the other animals – which has produced and will produce the greatest revolutions.

This conception of universal divinity sprang from his doctrine of Love. By love we can be at one with the divine power which he calls God. 'Love,' he says, 'is the true means by which the world is enjoyed: our love to others, and others' love to us.' Why, even the love of riches he excuses, since 'we love to be rich . . . that we thereby might be more greatly delightful.' And just as Richard Jefferies says that Felise loved before ever she loved a man, so Traherne says: 'That violence wherewith a man sometimes doteth upon one creature is but a little spark of that love, even toward all, which lurketh in his nature . . . When we dote upon the perfections and beauties of some one creature, we do not love that too much, but other things too little.' It is this love by which alone the commonwealth of all forms of life can be truly known, and men are like God when they are 'all life and mettle and vigour and love to everything,' and 'concerned and happy' in all things. His feeling of the interdependence of all the world is thus inseparable from his doctrine of love; love inspires it; by love alone can it be real and endure. 'He that is in all and with all can never be desolate.' And, nevertheless, he cannot always be thinking of the universe – he thought that the sun went round the earth – and just as he regards man as superior to other forms of life, so, perhaps, he has a filial love of 'this cottage of Heaven and Earth,' the brown land and blue sky, and one of the most beautiful of his meditations is where he says:

When I came into the country, and being seated among silent trees, and meads, and hills, had all my time in mine own hands, I resolved to spend it all, whatever it cost me, in the search of happiness, and to satiate that burning thirst which Nature had enkindled in me from my youth. In which I was so resolute, that I chose rather to live upon ten pounds a year, and go in leather clothes, and feed upon bread and water, so that I might have all my time clearly to myself, than to keep many thousands per annum in an estate of life where my time would be devoured in care and labour. And God was so pleased to accept of that desire, that from that time to this, I have had all things plentifully provided for me, without any care at all, my very study of Felicity making me more to prosper, than all the care in the whole world. So that through

His blessing I live a free and a kingly life as if the world were turned again into Eden, or much more, as it is at this day.

Traherne is remarkable in many ways, but for nothing more than for his mingling of man and nature in the celestial light of infancy. He begins, indeed, with the corn – the 'orient and immortal wheat' – but he goes on to the dust and stones and gates of the town, and then to the old men and the young men and the children. But it was only on 'some gilded cloud or flower' that Vaughan saw 'some shadows of eternity'; he longs to travel back to his childish time and to a city of the soul, but a shady city of palm-trees. Wordsworth, though he says that 'every common spirit' was 'apparell'd in celestial light' in his early childhood, only mentions 'meadow, grove and stream'; it is a tree, a single field, a flower, that reminds him of his loss; it is the fountains, meadows, hills and groves which he is anxious to assure of his lasting love. Perhaps many people's memories in this kind are of Nature more than of men. Even the social Lamb is at his deepest in recalling the child who was solitary in the great house and garden at Blakesmoor. With some reason for this priority of Nature is that her solitudes are the most rich. The presence of other children and of adults is comparatively commonplace, and in becoming, permanently or temporarily, part of a community, the spirit makes some sacrifice. Provided, then, that a child is happy and at ease in the solitude of Nature, it is more open than in company to what is afterwards regarded as spiritual intercourse. But above all, our memories of Nature are seldom or never flawed by the seeming triviality, the dislikes, the disgusts, the misunderstandings which give to memories of human society something of dulness and the commonplace. Thinking of ourselves and other children, we may also think of things which make idealization impossible. Thinking of ourselves in a great wood or field of flowers ever so long ago, it is hard not to exaggerate whatever give-and-take there was between the spirit of the child and the vast pure forces of the sun and the wind. In those days we did not see a tree as a column of a dark stony substance supporting a number of green wafers that live scarcely half a year, and grown for the manufacture of furniture, gates, and many other things; but we saw something quite unlike ourselves, large, gentle, of foreign tongue, without locomotion, yet full of the life and movement and sound of the leaves themselves, and also of the light, of the birds, and of the insects; and they were givers of a clear, deep joy that cannot be expressed. The brooding mind easily exalts this joy with the help of the disillusions and the knowledge and the folly and the thought of later years. A little time ago I heard of the death of one whom I had once seemed to know well, had roamed and talked and been silent with him, and I should have gone on doing so had he not gone far away and died. And when I heard of his death I kept on recalling his face and figure to my mind under familiar conditions, in the old rooms, by the same river, under the same elms. As before, I saw him in the clothes which he used to wear, smiling or laughing or perhaps grim. But wherever he was and whatever his look, there was always something – the shadow of a shadow, but awful

– in his face which made me feel that had I only seen it (and I felt that I ought to have seen it), in those days, I should have known he was to die early, with ambitions unfulfilled, far away.

And in this same way will the brain work in musing of earlier times. All that has come after deepens that candid brow of the child as a legend will darken a bright brook.

I once saw a girl of seven or eight years walking alone down a long grassy path in an old garden. On one hand rose a peaceful long slope of down; on the other, beyond the filberts, a high hedge shut out all but the pale blue sky, with white clouds resting on its lower mist like water-lilies on a still pool. Turning her back to the gabled house and its attendant beeches, she walked upon the narrow level path of perfect grass. The late afternoon sun fell full upon her, upon her brown head and her blue tunic, and upon the flowers of the borders at either side, the lowly white arabis foaming wild, the pansy, the white narcissus, the yellow jonquil and daffodil, the darker smouldering wallflowers, the tall yellow leopard's-bane, the tufts of honesty among the still dewy leaves of larkspur and columbine. But here and there, as she walked, the light was dimmed by the clusters of cool white humming cherry-blossom hanging out of the hot sky. In front of her the cherry trees seemed to meet and make a corridor of dark stems on either hand, paved green and white and gold, and roofed by milky white clouds that embowered the clear, wild warble of black-caps. Farther on, the flowers ceased and the grass was shadowed by new-leaved beeches, and at length involved in an uncertain mist of trees and shadows of trees, and there the cuckoo cried. For the child there was no end to the path.

She walked slowly, at first picking a narcissus or two, or stooping to smell a flower and letting her hair fall over it to the ground; but soon she was content only to brush the tips of the flowers with her outstretched hands, or, rising on tiptoe, to force her head up amongst the lowest branches of cherry-bloom. Then she did nothing at all but gravely walk on into the shadow and into Eternity, dimly foreknowing her life's days. She looked forward as one day she would look back over a broad sea of years, and in a drowsy, haunted gloom, full of the cuckoo's note, saw herself going always on and on among the interlacing shadows of tree trunks and branches and joys and pleasures and pains and sorrows that must have an end, she knew not how. She stopped, not venturing into that strange future under the beeches. She stared into the mist, where hovered the phantoms of the big girl, the young woman, the lover . . . which in turn she was to become. Under the last cherry tree something went out of her into the shadow, and those phantoms fed upon her blood as she stood still. But presently in the long beech corridors the gloom began to lighten and move and change to a glinting blue that approached her. 'Pee-oi,' shouted the peacock, now close at hand; 'pee-oi . . . pee-oi,' as he passed her by, and turning, she also shouted 'pee-oi,' frightening the cuckoo from the beeches, as she ran back among the flowers to the house.

What is to come of our Nature-teaching in schools?

What does it aim at? Whence does it arise? In part, no doubt, it is due to our desire to implant information. It is all very well for the poet to laugh –

> When Science has discovered something more
> We shall be happier than we were before;

but that is the road we are on at a high rate of speed. If we are fortunate we shall complete our inventory of the contents of heaven and earth by the time when the last man or woman wearing the last pair of spectacles has decided that, after all, it is a very good world and one which it is quite possible to live in. That, however, is an end which would not in itself be a sufficient inducement to push on towards it; still less can such a vision have set us upon the road.

Three things, perhaps, have more particularly persuaded us to pay our fare and mount for somewhere – three things which are really not to be sharply distinguished, though it is convenient to consider them separately. First, the literary and philosophical movement imperfectly described as the romantic revival and return to Nature of the eighteenth and nineteenth centuries. Poets and philosophers need private incomes, State porridge and what not, but literature and philosophy is a force, and for a century it has followed a course which was entered in the period of the French Revolution. This literature shows man in something like his true position in an infinite universe, and shows him particularly in his physical environment of sea, sky, mountain, rivers, woods, and other animals. Second, the enormous, astonishing, perhaps excessive, growth of towns, from which the only immediate relief is the pure air and sun of the country, a relief which is sought by the urban multitudes in large but insufficient numbers and for too short a time. Third, the triumph of science, of systematized observation. Helped, no doubt, by the force of industrialism – to which it gave help in return – science has had a great triumph. At one time it was supposed to have fatally undermined poetry, romance, religion, because it had confused the minds of some poets and critics.

These three things considered, Nature-study is inevitable. Literature sends us to Nature principally for joy, joy of the senses, of the whole frame, of the contemplative mind, and of the soul, joy which if it is found complete in these several ways might be called religious. Science sends us to Nature for knowledge. Industrialism and the great towns send us to Nature for health, that we may go on manufacturing efficiently, or, if we think right and have the power, that we may escape from it. But it would be absurd to separate joy, knowledge and health, except as we separate for convenience those things which have sent us out to seek for them; and Nature-teaching, if it is good, will never overlook one of these three. Joy, through knowledge, on a foundation of health, is what we appear to seek.

There is no longer any need to hesitate in speaking of joy in connection with schools, yet might we not still complain, as Thomas Traherne did two hundred and fifty years ago:

There was never a tutor that did professly teach Felicity, though that be the mistress of all other sciences. Nor did any of us study these things but as aliena, which we ought to have studied as our enjoyments. We studied to inform our Knowledge, but knew not for what end we so studied. And for lack of aiming at a certain end we erred in the manner.

If we cannot somehow have a professor of Felicity we are undone. Perhaps Nature herself will aid. Her presence will certainly make for felicity by enlarging her pupil for a time from the cloistered life which modern towns and their infinite conveniences and servitudes encourage. Tolstoy has said that in the open air 'new relations are formed between pupil and teacher: freer, simpler and more trustful'; and certainly his walk on a winter night with his pupils, chattering and telling tales (see *The School at Yasnaya Polyana*, by Leo Tolstoy), leaves an impression of electrical activity and felicity in the young and old minds of that party which is hardly to be surpassed. And how more than by Nature's noble and uncontaminated forms can a sense of beauty be nourished? Then, too, the reading of great poetry might well be associated with the study of Nature, since there is no great poetry which can be disseuered from Nature, while modern poets have all dipped their pens in the sunlight and wind and great waters, and appeal most to those who most resemble them in their loves. The great religious books, handed down to us by people who lived in closer intercourse with Nature than many of us, cannot be understood by indoor children and adults. Whether connected with this or that form of religion or not, whether taken as 'intimations of immortality' or not, the most profound and longest remembered feelings are often those derived from the contact of Nature with the child's mind.

Of health, though there are exactly as many physicians as patients, it is unnecessary to say anything, except that one of the pieces of knowledge – I do not speak of information – which science has left to us is that movement and the working of the brain in pure air and sunlight is good for body and soul, especially if joy is aiding.

Knowledge aids joy by discipline, by increasing the sphere of enjoyment, by showing us in animals, in plants, for example, what life is, how our own is related to theirs, showing us, in fact, our position, responsibilities and debts among the other inhabitants of the earth. Pursued out of doors where those creatures, moving and still, have their life and their beauty, knowledge is real. The senses are invited there to the subtlest and most delightful training, and have before them an immeasurable fresh field, not a field like that of books, full of old opinions, but one with which every eye and brain can have new vital intercourse. It is open to all to make discoveries as to the forms and habits of things, and care should be taken to preserve the child from the most verbose part of modern literature, that which repeats in multiplied ill-chosen words stale descriptions of birds and flowers, etc., coupled with trival fancies and insincere inventions. Let us not take the study, the lamp and the ink out of doors, as we used to take wild life – having killed it and placed it in spirits of wine – indoors. Let us also be careful to have knowledge as well as enthusiasm in our masters. Enthusiasm alone is not enthusiasm. There must, at some stage, be some anatomy, classification, pure brain-work; the teacher must be the equal in training of the mathematician, and he must be alive, which I never heard was a necessity for mathematicians. But not anatomy for all, perhaps; for some it might be impossible, and a study of colours, curves, perfumes, voices – a thousand things – might be substituted for it.

Yet Nature-study is not designed to produce naturalists, any more than music is taught in order to make musicians. If you produce nothing but naturalists you fail, and you will produce very few. The aim of study is to widen the culture of child and man, to do systematically what Mark Pattison tells us in his dry way he did for himself, by walking and outdoor sports, then – at the late age of seventeen – by collecting and reading such books as *The Natural History of Selborne*, and finally by a slow process of transition from natural history into 'the more abstract poetic emotion . . . a conscious and declared poetical sentiment and a devoted reading of the poets.' Geology did not come for another ten years, 'to complete the cycle of thought, and to give that intellectual foundation which is required to make the testimony of the eye, roaming over an undulating surface, fruitful and satisfying. When I came in after years to read *The Prelude* I recognized, as if it were my own history which was being told, the steps by which the love of the country boy for his hills and moors grew into poetical susceptibility for all imaginative presentations of beauty in every direction.' The botany, etc., would naturally be related to the neighbourhood of school or home; for there is no parish or district of which it might not be said, as Jefferies and Thoreau each said of his own, that it is a microcosm. By this means the natural history may easily be linked to a preliminary study of hill and valley and stream, the positions of houses, mills and villages, and the reasons for them, and the food supply, and so on, and this in turn leads on to – nay, involves – all that is most real in geography and history. The landscape retains the most permanent marks of the past, and a wise examination of it should evoke the beginnings of the majestic sentiment of our oneness with the future and the past, just as natural history should help to give the child a sense of oneness with all forms of life. To put it at its lowest, some such cycle of knowledge is needed if a generation that insists more and more on living in the country, or spending many weeks there, is not to be bored or to be compelled to entrench itself behind the imported amusements of the town.

15. The Inn

The night was dark and solid rain tumultuously invested the inn. As I stood in a dim passage I could see through the bar into the cloudy parlour, square and white, surrounded by settles, each curving about a round table made of one piece of elm on three legs. A reproduction of 'Rent Day' and a coloured picture of a bold Spanish beauty hung on the wall, which, for the rest, was sufficiently adorned by the sharp shadows of men's figures and furniture that mingled grotesquely. All the men but one leaned back upon the settles or forward upon the tables, their hands on their tankards, watching the one who sang a ballad – a ballad known to them so well that they seemed not to listen, but simply to let the melody surge about them and provoke what thoughts it would.

At some time, perhaps many times in his life, every man is likely to meet with a thing in art or nature or human life or books which astonishes and gives him a profound satisfaction, not so much because it is rich or beautiful or strange, as because it is a symbol of a thing which, without the symbol, he could never grasp and enjoy. The German archers making a target of Leonardo's sculptured horse and horseman at Milan; the glory of purple that has flown from a painted church window and settled upon a peasant's shoulders for an hour; the eloquence, as of an epigram rich in anger and woe, of one bare branch that juts out from a proud green wood into the little midnight stars and makes them smaller with its splendid pang; a woodman felling one by one the black and golden oak trees in the spring and slaying their ancient shadows; or, in a discreet and massive crowd, one jet of laughter, so full of joy or defiance or carelessness that it seems to cut through the heavy air like the whistle of a bullet – the world is one flame of these blossoms, could we but see. Music has many of them in her gift. Music, the rebel, the martyr, the victor – music, the romantic cry of matter striving to become spirit – is itself such a symbol, and there is no melody so poor that it will not at some time or another, to our watchful or receptive minds, have its festal hour in which it is crowned or at least crucified, for our solemn delight. 'Dolly Gray' I have heard sung all day by poor sluttish women as they gathered peas in the broad, burning fields of July, until it seemed that its terrible, acquiescent melancholy must have found a way to the stars and troubled them.

And of all music, the old ballads and folk songs and their airs are richest in the plain, immortal symbols. The best of them seem to be written in a language that should be universal, if only simplicity were truly simple to mankind. Their alphabet is small; their combinations are as the sunlight or the storm, and their words also are symbols. Seldom have they any direct relation to life as the realist believes it to be. They are poor in such detail as reveals a past age or a country not our own. They are in themselves epitomes of whole generations, of a whole countryside. They are the quintessence of many lives and passions made into a sweet cup for posterity. A myriad hearts and voices have in age after age poured themselves into the few notes and words. Doubtless, the old singers were not content, but we, who know them not, can well see in their old songs a kind of immortality for them in wanderings on the viewless air. The men and women – who hundreds of years ago were eating and drinking and setting their hearts on things – still retain a thin hold on life through the joy of us who hear and sing their songs, or tread their curving footpaths, or note their chisel marks on cathedral stones, or rest upon the undulating church-yard grass. The words, in league with a fair melody, lend themselves to infinite interpretations, according to the listener's heart. What great literature by known authors enables us to interpret thus by virtue of its subtlety, ballads and their music force us to do by their simplicity. The melody and the story or the song move us suddenly and launch us into an unknown. They are not art, they come to us imploring a new lease of life on the sweet earth, and so we come to give them something which the dull eye sees not in the words and notes themselves, out of our own hearts, as we do when we find a black hearthstone among the nettles, or hear the clangour of the joyous wild swan, invisible overhead, in the winter dawn.

In the parlour of the inn the singer stood up and sang of how a girl was walking alone in the meadows of spring when she saw a ship going out to sea and heard her true love crying on board; and he sailed to the wars and much he saw in strange countries, but never came back; and still she walks in the meadows and looks out to sea, though she is old, in the spring. He sang without stirring, without expression, except in so far as light and darkness from his own life emerged enmeshed among the deep notes. He might have been delivering an oracle of solemn but ambiguous things. And so in fact he was. By its simplicity and remoteness from life the song set going the potent logic of fancy which would lead many men to diverse conclusions. It excluded nothing of humanity except what baseness its melody might make impossible. The strangeness and looseness of its framework allowed each man to see himself therein, or some incident or dream in his life, or something possible to a self which he desired to be or imagined himself to be, or perhaps believed himself once to have been. There were no bounds of time or place. It included the love of Ruy Blas, of Marlowe, of Dante, of Catullus, of Kilhwch, of Swift, of Palomides, of Hazlitt, of Villon. . . . And that little inn, in the midst of mountains and immense night, seemed a temple of all souls, where a few faithful ones still burnt candles and remembered the dead.